United States Government Accountability Office

Report to Congressional Requesters

I0426418

March 2012

PRIVATE PENSIONS

Better Agency Coordination Could Help Small Employers Address Challenges to Plan Sponsorship

GAO
Accountability ★ Integrity ★ Reliability

PRIVATE PENSIONS

Better Agency Coordination Could Help Small Employers Address Challenges to Plan Sponsorship

GAO

Accountability * Integrity * Reliability

Highlights

Highlights of GAO-12-326, a report to congressional requesters

Why GAO Did This Study

Because about one-third of private-sector employees in the United States work for small employers, Congress and federal agencies have made efforts to encourage small employers to sponsor retirement plans for workers. However, federal data show workers' access to plans remains limited, leaving many without a work-based plan to save for retirement. For this report, GAO examined (1) characteristics of small employers that are more or less likely to sponsor a plan for their employees, (2) challenges small employers face in establishing and maintaining a plan for their employees, and (3) options to address these challenges and attract more small employer plan sponsors.

GAO defined small employers as for-profit firms that employ 100 or fewer employees. GAO analyzed Internal Revenue Service (IRS) and Department of Labor (Labor) data, interviewed agency officials and experts, held discussion groups with small employers, and reviewed relevant federal rules, literature, and retirement plan proposals.

What GAO Recommends

GAO recommends that Labor convene an interagency task force with Treasury, IRS, and SBA to coordinate existing research, education, and outreach efforts to foster small employer plan sponsorship. GAO also recommends that IRS consider modifying tax forms to gather complete, reliable information about SEP IRAs. Agencies generally agreed with GAO's recommendations; however, Labor disagreed with GAO's recommendation to create a single webportal for federal guidance. However, because federal resources are scattered across different sites, GAO believes consolidating plan information onto one webportal could benefit small employers.

View GAO-12-326. For more information, contact Charles Jeszeck at (202) 512-7215 or jeszeckc@gao.gov .

What GAO Found

Based on available data, about 14 percent of small employers sponsor some type of retirement plan. Overall, GAO found that the likelihood that a small employer will sponsor a retirement plan largely depends on the size of the employer's workforce and the workers' average wages more than on the industry in which the employer operates and the geographic region in which the employer is located. GAO found the greatest likelihood of plan sponsorship was among small employers with larger numbers of employees and those paying an average annual wage of $50,000 to $99,999. GAO also found that the most common plans sponsored by small employers are 401(k)s and Savings Incentive Match Plans for Employees (SIMPLE) Individual Retirement Arrangements (IRA)—an employer-sponsored IRA designed for small employers—at 46 percent and 40 percent, respectively, of total plans. However, IRS currently does not have the means to collect information on employers that sponsor another type of IRA plan designed for small employers, the Simplified Employee Pension (SEP) IRA plan, which limits what is known about employers that sponsor these plans.

Small employers and retirement experts identified several challenges to starting and maintaining retirement plans. Many small employers said they feel overwhelmed by the number of retirement plan options, administration requirements, and fiduciary responsibilities. For example, many are concerned about the potential risks associated with sponsoring a plan. Although federal agencies conduct education and outreach on retirement plans, a number of small employers and other stakeholders said small employers were unaware of these initiatives. For example, Labor, IRS, and the Small Business Administration (SBA) collaborate to develop and disseminate information and guidance online but do so through separate websites and in a largely uncoordinated fashion. Small employers and other stakeholders also cited other challenges to plan sponsorship, including a lack of financial resources, time, and personnel. However, some small employers said their employees prioritized health benefits over retirement benefits. To address some of the challenges to plan sponsorship, some small employers said they use contracted service providers that perform plan administration tasks.

Small employers and other stakeholders offered options for addressing some challenges and reducing the complexity of plan sponsorship for small employers. Options included simplification of federal requirements for plan administration, such as easing or eliminating certain plan testing requirements. Some stakeholders said increasing the tax credit for plan startup costs could further defray costs and help boost plan sponsorship. Some stakeholders also said that the federal government could conduct more education and outreach efforts to inform small employers about plans. Pension reform proposals in the United States, along with certain features of pension systems in other countries, may provide additional options that could increase plan sponsorship and increase workers' access to retirement plans. For example, asset pooling is a feature that allows small employers to pool resources for economies of scale, which can lower plan costs. In light of the variety of options, Labor, the Department of the Treasury, IRS, and SBA should jointly evaluate existing options and develop new proposals with the goal of mitigating barriers to small employer plan sponsorship.

_____ United States Government Accountability Office

Contents

Tables

Figures

Abbreviations

ACT	Advisory Committee on Tax Exempt and Government Entities
AICPA	American Institute of Certified Public Accountants
ASPPA	American Society of Pension Professionals & Actuaries
BLS	Bureau of Labor Statistics
CDW	Compliance Data Warehouse
CPS	Current Population Survey
CRS	Congressional Research Service
DB	defined benefit
DC	defined contribution
EGTRRA	Economic Growth and Tax Relief Reconciliation Act of 2001
EIN	employer identification number
ERISA	Employee Retirement Income Security Act of 1974
IRA	Individual Retirement Arrangement
IRC	Internal Revenue Code
IRP	Information Returns Processing
IRS	Internal Revenue Service
Labor	Department of Labor
NAICS	North American Industry Classification System
NCS	National Compensation Survey
NEST	National Employment Savings Trust
PBGC	Pension Benefit Guaranty Corporation
SARSEP	Salary Reduction Simplified Employee Pension
SBA	Small Business Administration
SEP	Simplified Employee Pension
SIMPLE	Savings Incentive Match Plans for Employees

March 5, 2012

The Honorable Herb Kohl
Chairman
Special Committee on Aging
United States Senate

The Honorable Michael B. Enzi
Ranking Member
Committee on Health, Education, Labor,
   and Pensions
United States Senate

The Honorable Jeff Bingaman
United States Senate

About 42 million workers, or about one-third of all private-sector employees, work for small employers, and recent federal data suggest many of these workers lack access to a work-based retirement plan to save for retirement. An estimated 51 percent to 71 percent of workers at employers with fewer than 100 workers do not have access to a work-based retirement plan compared to an estimated 19 percent to 35 percent of those who work for employers with 100 or more workers.[1]

Over the years, the federal government has taken steps to encourage small employers to sponsor retirement plans, and Congress has enacted legislation that has established incentives such as plan types with fewer federal reporting requirements, higher plan contribution limits, and a tax credit for plan startup costs. The Department of Labor (Labor) and the Department of the Treasury's (Treasury) Internal Revenue Service (IRS) have also increased education and outreach to these employers. However, small employers continue to face a number of barriers to starting and maintaining plans for their workers. In 2008, GAO reported on challenges that can limit small employer sponsorship of Individual

---

[1] The lower percentages in these ranges are Labor's Bureau of Labor Statistics' (BLS) estimates based on 2011 data from the National Compensation Survey. The higher percentages are the Employee Benefit Research Institute's (EBRI) estimates based on 2011 data from the Census Bureau's Current Population Survey. For more information on these ranges, see appendix I.

Retirement Arrangement (IRA)[2] plans, including administrative costs, contribution requirements, and eligibility based on employee tenure and compensation, among others.[3] Other research also suggests that a difficult economy and concerns about the overall cost of retirement plans may be factors for some small employers that are less likely to sponsor plans. For example, a recent survey found that difficult business conditions were a top reason employers reported for being unlikely to sponsor a retirement plan.[4]

Certain characteristics associated with small employers may also contribute to the challenges of starting and maintaining a plan. When compared with large employers, small employers are more likely to encounter higher rates of employee turnover and higher costs per employee to comply with federal regulations. Further, small employers—especially start-ups—rely heavily on owner investment and bank credit, and operating revenue can be uncertain from year to year.[5] Federal data suggest that about half of all new businesses (nearly all of which are small) do not survive for more than 5 years. All these conditions can make it difficult for small employers to focus on providing retirement benefits for their workers.

---

[2]An IRA is a personal retirement savings arrangement that offers certain tax advantages and allows individuals to set aside money for retirement into an individual account, or purchase an annuity contract. IRAs can be employer-sponsored or maintained by an individual.

[3]GAO, *Individual Retirement Accounts: Government Actions Could Encourage More Employers to Offer IRAs to Employees*, GAO-08-590 (Washington, D.C.: June 4, 2008).

[4]Transamerica Center for Retirement Studies, *12th Annual Retirement Survey* (July 2011).

[5]Previous work by GAO has discussed revenue uncertainty among small employers as a factor in low rates of plan sponsorship. For more information, see GAO, *Pension Plans: Characteristics of Persons in the Labor Force Without Pension Coverage*, GAO/HEHS-00-131(Washington, D.C.: Aug. 22, 2000).

In light of these ongoing challenges, GAO was asked to examine issues related to retirement plan sponsorship among small employers.[6] We answered the following questions:

- What characteristics are associated with small employers that are more likely or less likely to sponsor a retirement plan for their employees?

- What challenges do small employers face in establishing and maintaining a retirement plan for their employees? and

- What options exist to address these challenges and attract more small employer plan sponsors?

To answer these research questions, we combined and analyzed retirement plan data from Labor and IRS data on 5.3 million small employers.[7] We performed regression analyses to identify characteristics of small employers that are most likely to sponsor plans. We conducted literature reviews and interviewed retirement experts, organizations representing small employers, agency officials, and others on challenges faced by small employers in establishing and maintaining plans, and options for addressing those challenges. In addition, we conducted structured interviews with groups of small employers that did and did not sponsor plans. These interviews were conducted in five cities, which were judgmentally selected for geographic diversity.[8] We also reviewed relevant federal laws and regulations. Additional details regarding our methodology can be found in appendix I. We conducted this performance audit from October 2010 to March 2012 in accordance with generally accepted government auditing standards. Those standards require that we plan and perform the audit to obtain sufficient, appropriate evidence to provide a reasonable basis for our findings and conclusions based on our

---

[6]GAO limited the scope of this study to employer-sponsored plans and did not examine work-based retirement plans that are offered through but not sponsored by the employer or retirement plans maintained by individuals outside of the workplace. Further, since the report's focus was on the employer, GAO did not examine the participation rates of the employees at small employers as this was also considered outside the scope of this report.

[7]For the purposes of this study, GAO defined a small employer as a for-profit firm with least 1 employee and no more than 100 employees. For more information, see appendix I.

[8]The five cities were Atlanta, Boston, Chicago, Los Angeles, and Washington, D.C.

audit objectives. We believe that the evidence obtained provides a reasonable basis for our findings and conclusions based on our audit objectives.

Background

To encourage employers to establish and maintain retirement plans for their employees, the federal government provides preferential tax treatment under the Internal Revenue Code (IRC) for plans that meet certain requirements.[9] In addition, the Employee Retirement Income Security Act of 1974 (ERISA), as amended, sets forth certain protections for participants in private-sector retirement plans and establishes standards of conduct for those that manage the plans and their assets, generally called fiduciaries.[10] To the extent they qualify as fiduciaries under the law,[11] plan sponsors assume certain responsibilities and potential liability under ERISA. For example, a fiduciary must act prudently and solely in the interest of plan participants and their beneficiaries, which may require documenting decisions relating to the plan, including hiring outside professionals or service providers that advise and help administer plans. Small employers may choose a plan for their employees from one of three categories: employer-sponsored IRA plans; defined contribution (DC) plans; and defined benefit (DB) plans (often referred to as traditional pension plans).[12] Appendix II presents

---

[9]The Internal Revenue Code (IRC) establishes requirements that private retirement plans must satisfy, including minimum coverage and benefits, in order to qualify for favorable tax treatment. Employers that sponsor these tax-qualified plans are entitled to a deduction (within limits) for the contributions they make, and contributions are not included in an employee's income until benefits are received. IRS enforces the IRC requirements that apply to tax-qualified plans.

[10]Pub. L. No. 93-406, 88 Stat. 829, 874.

[11]ERISA requires plans to have at least one named fiduciary who manages plan operation and administration, and other individuals may qualify as fiduciaries based on their function. For example, a person who exercises any discretionary authority or control over the management of the plan or any control over the assets is considered a fiduciary under ERISA. 29 U.S.C. § 1002(21); see also 29 C.F.R. § 2510.3-21. For more information about the fiduciary requirements, see 29 U.S.C. §§ 1101-14 and 29 C.F.R. part 2550. Labor enforces the fiduciary responsibility standards and certain other ERISA requirements, such as reporting and disclosure requirements. In 2010, Labor's Employee Benefits Security Administration proposed expanding the regulatory definition of "fiduciary," 75 Fed. Reg. 65,263 (Oct. 22, 2010), but in 2011, the agency announced plans to repropose the rule after further analysis and additional public input.

[12]In this report, we use the term "pension" to refer generally to all types of private retirement plans, not just DB plans.

information provided by Labor and IRS about some of the various types of retirement savings plans available to small employers.

Employer-sponsored IRA plans: Employer-sponsored IRA plans allow employers and, in some cases, employees to make contributions for deposit in separate IRA accounts for each participating employee. These plans generally have fewer administration and reporting requirements than other types of plans. Participating employees bear the full investment risk of their account assets. There are two types of employer-sponsored IRA plans. Savings Incentive Match Plans for Employees (SIMPLE)[13] IRA plans require employers to either match their eligible employees' voluntary salary reductions (typically up to 3 percent of compensation) or to contribute 2 percent of compensation for each eligible employee. The second type is the Simplified Employee Pension (SEP) IRA plan,[14] which can be sponsored by an employer of any size, and has higher employer contribution limits than the SIMPLE IRA plan. In a SEP IRA plan, employer contributions are voluntary and employee salary reductions are not permitted.[15]

Defined contribution plans: DC plans allow employers, employees, or both to contribute to individual employee accounts that are grouped under a single plan. Employee salary reductions, if provided under the plan, may be pretax or after-tax, in some cases. As with employer-sponsored IRA plans, employees participating in DC plans bear the full risk of investment and will realize any returns (gains or losses) on those investments. DC plans tend to have higher limits for employee contributions but also more rules and reporting requirements than

---

[13]26 U.S.C. § 408(p). SIMPLE IRA plans are available to employers that do not sponsor another type of qualified plan and have 100 or fewer employees who meet certain minimum compensation requirements. All employees who have received at least $5,000 in compensation during the preceding 2 calendar years and are reasonably expected to receive at least $5,000 in compensation during the current year must be eligible to participate.

[14]26 U.S.C. § 408(k).

[15]Employee salary reductions under SEP IRA plans were eliminated beginning in 1997. However, SEP IRA plans established prior to 1997 whose plan terms permitted salary reductions—a plan called a Salary Reduction Simplified Employee Pension Plan (SARSEP)—may continue to offer salary reductions. 26 U.S.C. § 408(k)(6)(H).

employer-sponsored IRA plans.[16] For example, some DC plans may be required to conduct annual testing in order to ensure that the contributions or benefits provided under the plan do not discriminate against rank-and-file workers in favor of highly compensated employees,.[17] In addition to nondiscrimination testing, some DC plans may also be subject to top-heavy requirements and be required to conduct further testing to ensure a minimum level of benefits are provided to rank-and-file workers in plans that are sponsored by owner-dominated firms, where the majority of benefits accrue to "key" employees, such as owners and top executives.[18] As we have previously reported, top-heavy requirements are intended to address a greater potential for tax-shelter abuses in such plans.[19] Top-heavy requirements are most likely to affect smaller plans (fewer than 100 participants), according to the IRS. The

---

[16]Most tax-qualified plans are required to annually file Form 5500, developed jointly by Labor, IRS, and the Pension Benefit Guaranty Corporation to satisfy the annual reporting requirements under ERISA and the IRC. ERISA established a reporting and disclosure framework, in part, to protect the interests of participants and beneficiaries by requiring that certain financial and other information be provided to participants and beneficiaries, as well as to the federal government. Some small plans may be eligible to use a simplified version of Form 5500. SIMPLE IRA plans and SEP IRA plans that comply with certain alternative methods of compliance are not required to file Form 5500.

[17]See 26 U.S.C. § 401(a)(4); 26 C.F.R. §§ 1.401(a)(4)-1 through 1.401(a)(4)-4.

[18]26 U.S.C. § 416. In general, a plan is top-heavy if the accumulated contributions or benefits of key employees exceed 60 percent of the accumulated contributions or benefits all employees under the plan. Key employees include certain owners and officers of the employer whose annual compensation exceeds a specified amount. If a plan is determined to be top heavy, it must make certain adjustments to maintain its tax-qualified status, such as providing higher minimum contributions to nonkey employees than would otherwise be required. Other plans subject to top-heavy requirements include DB plans and SEP IRA plans.

[19]The definition of a key employee for purposes of top-heavy testing—as opposed to the definition of a highly compensated employee for purposes of general nondiscrimination testing—emphasizes firm ownership because in small, owner-dominated firms, compensation may not be a reliable indicator of who controls the firm and the pension plan design. Without identifying key employees, owners of smaller family-owned firms could manipulate assignments and salaries to avoid top-heavy status and exclude nonfamily workers from top-heavy benefits. For more information, see GAO, *Private Pensions: "Top-Heavy" Rules for Owner-Dominated Plans*, GAO/HEHS-00-141 (Washington, D.C., Sept. 29, 2000).

most common type of DC plan is a 401(k) plan.[20] In 401(k) plans, employees can defer a portion of their salary—pretax or after tax, if permitted by the plan—for deposit into a separate retirement account. Employers may also choose to make additional contributions (such as contributing a percentage of each eligible employee's salary), match the amount contributed by the employee, or both. One type of 401(k) plan, the safe harbor 401(k) plan, is not subject to some of the requirements associated with traditional 401(k)s that generally require annual plan testing. However, under safe harbor 401(k) plans, employers are required to make certain contributions to each participant's account.[21] Another type of tax-qualified DC plan, the profit sharing plan, gives the employer the discretion to determine annually whether and how much to pay into the plan, within certain maximum limits. Employer contributions, if any, are allocated to each employee according to the terms of the plan.

Defined benefit plans: Unlike employer-sponsored IRA and DC plans, sponsors of DB plans promise to provide a retirement benefit of a specified amount that is typically based on factors such as an employee's years of service and, often, salary. The benefits in private-sector DB plans are generally protected against an employer's inability to pay, within certain limitations, by federal insurance provided through the Pension Benefit Guaranty Corporation (PBGC).[22] The employer is generally responsible for funding the plan[23] and may be responsible for investing and managing its assets. In a DB plan, the employer bears all investment risk. DB plans are also generally subject to ERISA reporting

---

[20]26 U.S.C. § 401(k). Although a 401(k) arrangement is a plan feature, for purposes of this report we classified it as a plan type. Different features of 401(k) plans are also available—such as safe harbor 401(k) plans, automatic enrollment 401(k) plans, and SIMPLE 401(k) plans, which are generally subject to the same requirements as SIMPLE IRA plans.

[21]26 U,S,C, § 401(k)(12). Safe harbor 401(k) plans require employers to either make a specified matching contribution to each participating employee's account or contribute at least 3 percent of compensation to all nonhighly compensated eligible employees.

[22]The assets held in DC plans and employer-sponsored IRA plans are not insured by the Pension Benefit Guaranty Corporation.

[23]Employee contributions sometimes are required as well, but the employer is generally responsible for the balance of the funding requirements, including from the effects of plan experience differing from the actuarial assumptions. Most private sector DB plans do not require any employee contributions, while most public sector DB plans do.

requirements, nondiscrimination testing, and top-heavy requirements. Operating DB plans typically requires the expertise of an actuary.

Over the years, Congress has responded to concerns about lack of access to workplace retirement plans for employees of small businesses with legislation to lower costs, simplify requirements, and ease administrative burden. For example, The Revenue Act of 1978[24] and the Small Business Job Protection Act of 1996[25] established the SEP IRA plan and the SIMPLE IRA plan respectively, featuring fewer compliance requirements than other plan types. The Economic Growth and Tax Relief Reconciliation Act of 2001 (EGTRRA)[26] also included a number of provisions that affected small businesses. For example, EGTRRA eliminated top-heavy testing requirements for safe harbor 401(k)s, increased contribution limits for employer-sponsored IRA plans and 401(k) plans, and created a tax credit for small employers to offset startup costs, including the cost of educating employees about a new plan.[27] EGTRRA also created a tax credit for individuals within certain income limits who make eligible contributions to retirement plans. The Pension Protection Act of 2006,[28] among other changes, made these EGTRRA provisions permanent and established additional provisions that support retirement plan participation by rank-and-file employees, such as automatic enrollment.

To help encourage plan sponsorship, federal agencies conduct education and outreach activities and provide information about retirement plans for small employers. Labor, IRS, and the Small Business Administration

---

[24]Pub. L. No. 95-600, § 152, 92 Stat. 2763, 2791.

[25]Pub. L. No. 104-188, § 1421, 110 Stat. 1755, 1792.

[26]Pub. L. No. 107-16, 115 Stat. 38.

[27]The credit for small employer pension plan startup costs applies to certain startup costs in connection with the establishment of a new qualified DB plan, DC plan (including 401(k) plans), SIMPLE IRA plan, or SEP IRA plan. To be eligible, an employer must have no more than 100 employees who received at least $5,000 of compensation in the preceding year. The credit equals 50 percent of qualified startup costs, which include administration costs and employee education, up to a maximum of $500 per year (for the first 3 years of the plan). 26 U.S.C. § 45E.

[28]Pub. L. No. 109-280, 120 Stat. 780. EGTRRA was set to expire on December 31, 2010, but the Pension Protection Act of 2006 made permanent EGTRRA's provisions relating to pensions and IRAs.

(SBA)—which maintains an extensive network of field offices—have collaborated with each other and with national and local organizations to develop information on small employer retirement plans[29] and conduct outreach with small employers. For example, Labor, IRS, SBA and the U.S. Chamber of Commerce partnered to create the Choosing a Retirement Solution Campaign, which targets small employers and their employees.[30] The campaign's educational materials, including web-based retirement plan guidance for small employers, highlight key aspects of and differences between various plans and features, including tax benefits for employers and employees. Labor also worked with the Society for Human Resource Management and the American Institute of Certified Public Accountants (AICPA) on the Fiduciary Education Campaign to provide retirement plan fiduciaries with information about their fiduciary responsibilities under ERISA.

In addition, various private-sector service providers, from individual accountants, investment advisers, recordkeepers, and actuaries to insurance companies and banks, assist sponsors with their retirement plans. Some sponsors hire a single provider that offers a range of plan services for one fee—sometimes referred to as a "bundled" services arrangement. Other sponsors hire different providers for individual services under an "unbundled" arrangement, paying a separate fee for each service. Plan services include legal, accounting, trustee/custodial, recordkeeping, investment management, and investment education or advice. Service providers can also assist with plan administration functions, including nondiscrimination testing, top-heavy testing, and filing of government reports. Some providers also include payroll services, which further centralize an employer's administrative services through a single company. Labor provides some guidance for plan sponsors in selecting and monitoring plan service providers.[31] Further, the American

---

[29]Labor, IRS, and PBGC have a Memorandum of Understanding on enhancing coordination with respect to the funding of any pension plan in connection with certain provisions of ERISA and the IRC, which includes sharing information when coordinated administrative and enforcement action concerning a specific matter is in the government interest.

[30]U.S. Department of Labor, *Retirement Savings Education Campaign*, accessed January 16, 2012, http://www.dol.gov/EBSA/savingmatters.html.

[31]U.S. Department of Labor, *Fact Sheet: Tips for Selecting and Monitoring Service Providers For Your Employee Benefit Plan* (disseminated May 2004), accessed January 13, 2012, http://www.dol.gov/ebsa/newsroom/fs052505.html.

Society of Pension Professionals & Actuaries (ASPPA) publishes a list of certified firms that adhere to ASPPA's standards and best practices concerning recordkeeping and administration services for retirement plans.

Number of Employees and Average Pay Level Greatly Influence Plan Sponsorship

More Employees and Higher Average Wages Increase the Likelihood of Plan Sponsorship

GAO found that the number of employees and average wages greatly influence the likelihood that a small employer will sponsor a retirement plan.[32] Further, the regression analysis using Labor and IRS data found that small employers with larger numbers of employees were the most likely of all small employers to sponsor a retirement plan, as were those paying average annual wages of $50,000 to $99,999. Conversely, employers with the fewest employees and the lowest average annual wages were very unlikely to sponsor a retirement plan.

A separate GAO analysis using Labor and IRS data found an overall small employer sponsorship rate of 14 percent in 2009.[33] However, the sponsorship rate does not include small employers that sponsor SEP IRA plans because IRS currently does not have a means to collect these data, which limits what is known about small employers that sponsor SEP

---

[32]Several experts stated that a firm's age could also affect the likelihood of plan sponsorship, with newer employers less likely to sponsor a plan. However, our analysis was unable to address the number of years in operation due to technical challenges. See appendix I for further discussion of the technical challenges.

[33]The sponsorship rate cited in this report is limited to single employers that sponsor a plan. As a consequence, the sponsorship rate does not include small employers that participated only in multiple employer retirement plans or multiemployer retirement plans, which are outside the scope of this report. GAO is currently conducting ongoing work on multiple employer plans and multiemployer plans and their role in the private pension system. For further information on the scope of GAO's analysis, see Appendix I.

plans. According to IRS, its Form 5498, "IRA Contribution Information,"[34] includes some SEP information; however, the agency is unable to link this information to an employer's employer identification number (EIN). As a result, IRS can identify participants in SEP plans but not sponsoring employers.[35] While the IRS Tax Forms and Publication Committee proposed a change to the form to allow IRS to identify SEP IRA plan sponsors, officials said the proposal was not adopted.

Further examination of sponsorship rates looking at small employer characteristics found that those with 26 to 100 employees had the highest sponsorship rate—31 percent—while small employers with 1 to 4 employees had the lowest rate—5 percent (see fig. 1). Additionally, even though small employers with 26 to 100 employees made up only 10 percent of the overall small employer population, they sponsored more retirement plans than employers with 1 to 4 employees.

---

[34]Plan issuers or trustees of IRA plans submit form 5498 to IRS and to IRA participants each year to report annual contribution and other information for each account. Form 5498 shows the issuer or trustee's employer identification number as well as the participant's Social Security Number. A copy of IRS Form 5498 can be found in appendix III.

[35]Additionally, whereas IRS collects information from employers about SIMPLE employee contributions on Form W-2 filed for each employee, employers do not separately identify SEP information on an employee's W-2.

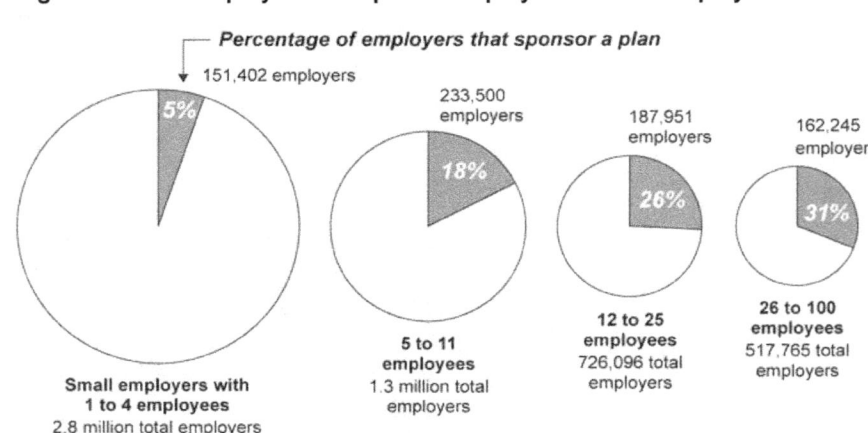

Figure 1: Small Employer Plan Sponsorship by Number of Employees in 2009

Percentage of employers that sponsor a plan

151,402 employers

5%

Small employers with
1 to 4 employees
2.8 million total employers

233,500
employers

18%

5 to 11
employees
1.3 million total
employees

187,951
employers

26%

12 to 25
employees
726,096 total
employers

162,245
employers

31%

26 to 100
employees
517,765 total
employers

Source: GAO analysis of Labor and IRS data.

Looking at the average annual wage characteristics, small employers with average annual wages of $50,000 to $99,999 had the highest rate of retirement plan sponsorship at 34 percent while small employers with average wages of under $10,000 had the lowest sponsorship rate—3 percent (see fig. 2). Further, despite having a smaller overall population, small employers with average annual wages of $50,000 to $99,999 sponsor almost three times as many retirement plans compared to small employers paying average wages of under $10,000. As a point of comparison, the overall annual average wages for employees working for small employers was about $38,000.

Figure 2: Small Employer Plan Sponsorship by Average Annual Employee Wage in 2009

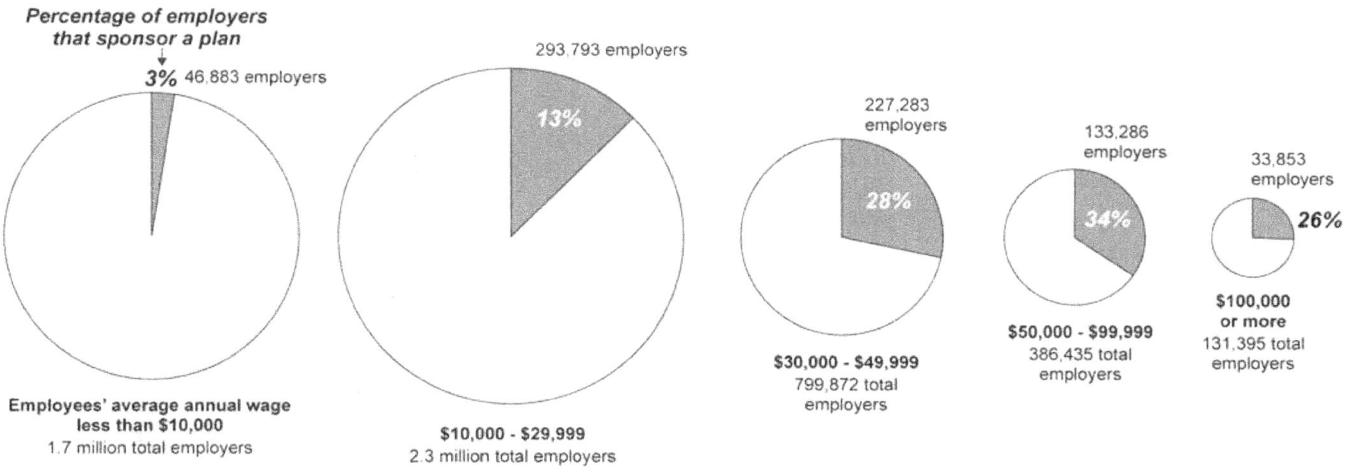

Percentage of employers that sponsor a plan

3% 46,883 employers

Employees' average annual wage less than $10,000
1.7 million total employers

293,793 employers
13%

$10,000 - $29,999
2.3 million total employers

227,283 employers
28%

$30,000 - $49,999
799,872 total employers

133,286 employers
34%

$50,000 - $99,999
386,435 total employers

33,853 employers
26%

$100,000 or more
131,395 total employers

Source: GAO analysis of Labor and IRS data.

Analysis of the Labor and IRS data examining the interaction between both characteristics—number of employees and average annual wages—illustrates how sponsorship rates increase as numbers of employees and average annual wages increase. For example, the plan sponsorship rate for employers with 26 to 100 employees and average wages of $30,000 to $49,999 was more than nine times higher than employers with the same number of employees and wages below $10,000. Further, the sponsorship rate for small employers with 26 to 100 employees exceeded 75 percent when average wages were $50,000 or higher. In contrast, small employers with 1 to 4 employees reached their highest sponsorship rate of 13 percent when average annual wages were $50,000 or more; however, sponsorship rates were still about one-sixth the rate for small employers with 26 to 100 employees in the same wage category. Our analysis showed the sponsorship rate for employers with one to four employees lowered the overall sponsorship rate in the average annual wage categories. For example, the figure shows that small employers with average annual wages of $100,000 or more have an overall sponsorship rate of 26 percent, but this is much lower than the sponsorship rates for small employers with five or more employees. Figure 3 shows small employer sponsorship rates by size of employer and average annual wage paid.

Figure 3: Small Employer Plan Sponsorship Rate by Employees' Average Annual Wage and Number of Employees in 2009

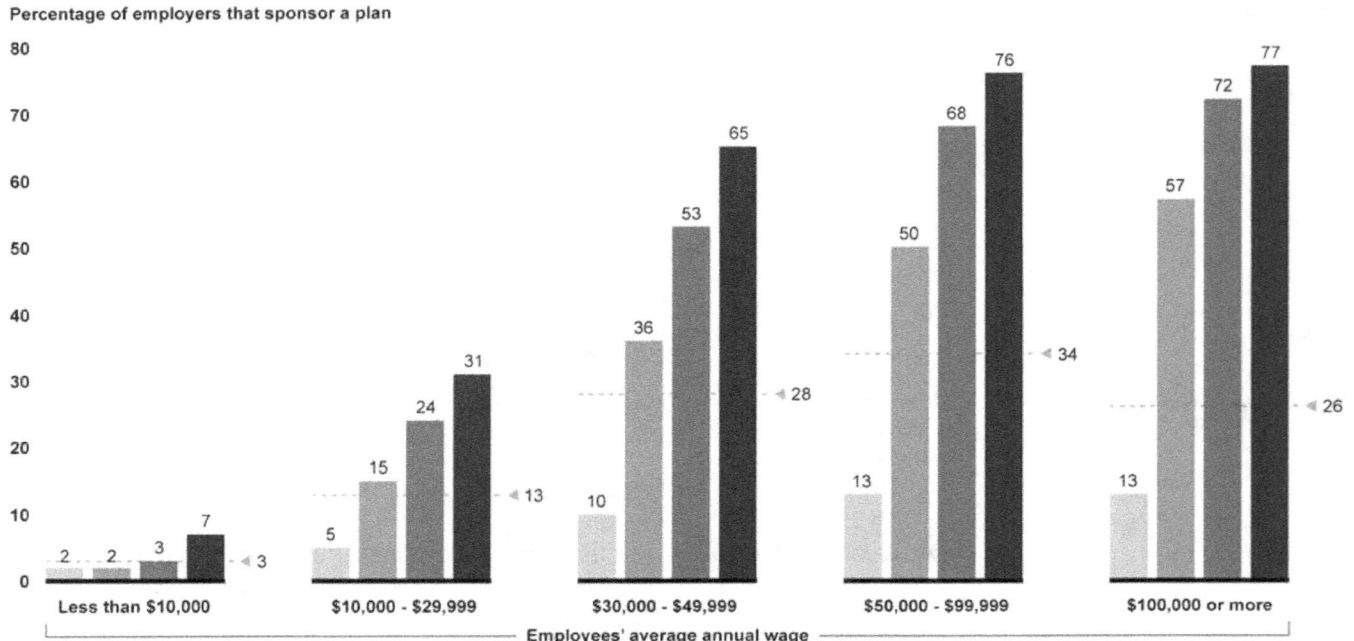

Percentage of employers that sponsor a plan

Employees' average annual wage

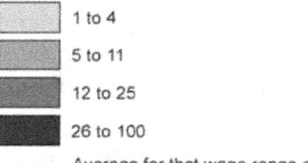

Size of employer (total employees)

- 1 to 4
- 5 to 11
- 12 to 25
- 26 to 100

- - - - Average for that wage range among all small employers

Source: GAO analysis of Labor and IRS data.

In examining the geographic distribution of sponsorship rates, small employers in the Midwest and Northeast were more likely to sponsor plans, while employers in the West and South were less likely.[36] Further, in examining data on individual states, Connecticut, Wisconsin, and Washington, D.C., had the highest rate—with Washington, D.C., showing the top rate of 23 percent. Florida and Mississippi had the lowest

[36]For purposes of this analysis, we used geographic regions used by the Census Bureau. For a list of states included in each region, see appendix V.

sponsorship rates at fewer than 10 percent. Figure 4 shows the percentage of small employers that sponsor plans by state.[37]

Figure 4: Small Employer Plan Sponsorship by State in 2009

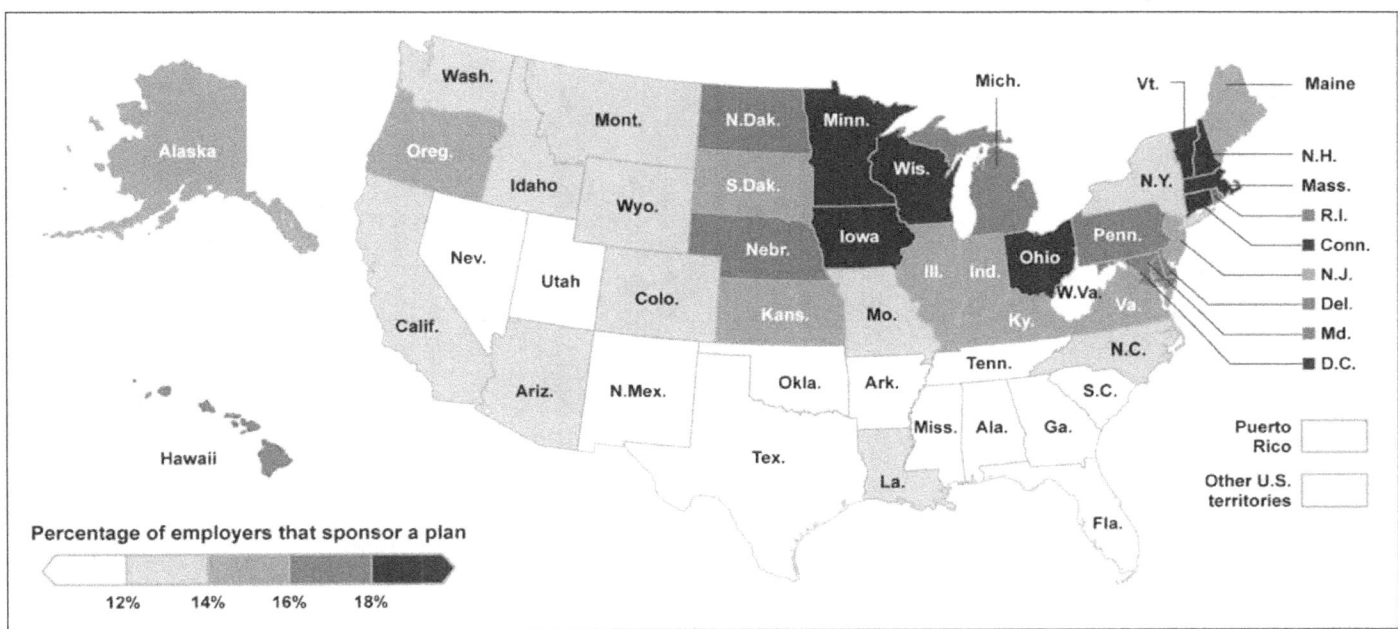

Source: GAO analysis of Labor and IRS data

401(k)s and SIMPLE IRAs Were the Most Common Plan Types

According to GAO analysis of Labor and IRS data, 401(k) and SIMPLE IRA plans were overwhelmingly the most common types of plans sponsored by small employers. Out of slightly more than 712,000 small employers that sponsored a single type of plan, about 86 percent sponsored either a 401(k) or a SIMPLE IRA plan.[38] Additionally, non-401(k) DC plans, which include non-401(k) profit sharing plans, make up 11 percent of the plan type population; SARSEP IRAs are 3 percent, while DB plans make up only about 1 percent of the small employer

---

[37]For a complete list of sponsorship rates in each state, see appendix V.

[38]Three percent of the small employer population sponsored multiple plans; however, these small employers were excluded from the plan type analysis. For a further discussion of this limitation, see appendix I.

sponsor population.[39] Figure 5 shows the proportion of plan types sponsored by small employers.

Figure 5: Small Employer Plan Sponsorship by Plan Type in 2009

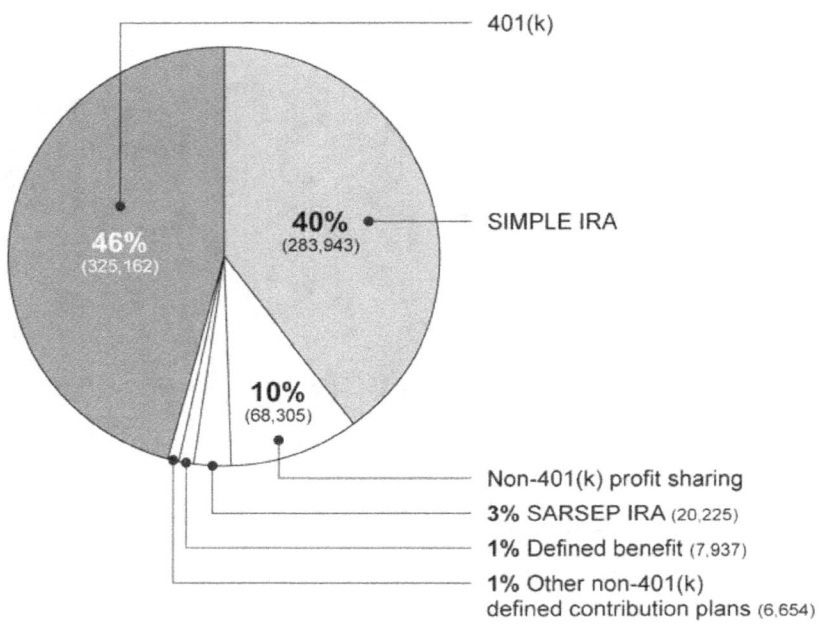

Source: GAO analysis of Labor and IRS data.

Note: Percentages do not add up to 100 due to rounding.

In examining the characteristics of small employers that sponsored the two most common plan types, SIMPLE IRA plan sponsors outnumbered 401(k) plan sponsors when small employers had fewer employees (see fig. 6). For example, looking at small employers with 1 to 11 employees that sponsored plans, there were 43 percent more SIMPLE IRA plans than there were 401(k) plans. In contrast, for small employers with 12 to 100 employees that sponsored plans, there were 90 percent more 401(k) plans than SIMPLE IRA plans.

---

[39]A SARSEP plan is a type of SEP IRA plan set up before 1997 that permits employee salary reduction contributions. Employee salary reductions under SEP IRA plans were eliminated beginning in 1997; however, SARSEP plans established prior to 1997 may continue to offer salary reductions. 26 U.S.C. § 408(k)(6)(H).

Figure 6: Percentage of Small Employer 401(k) Plan Sponsors and SIMPLE IRA Plan Sponsors by Number of Employees in 2009

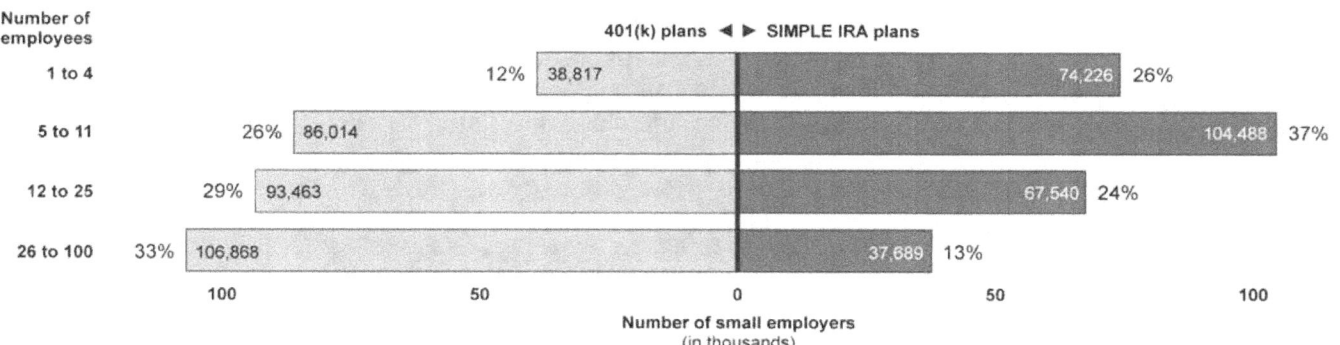

Source: GAO analysis of Labor and IRS data

Similarly, in looking at small employers by average annual wages, there were 61 percent more SIMPLE IRA plans than 401(k) plans for those with employees who had average annual wages under $30,000. In contrast, for employers with employees who had average annual wages of $30,000 or more, there were more than double the numbers of 401(k) plans than SIMPLE IRA plans. See figure 7 for the percentage of small employer 401(k) plan sponsors and SIMPLE IRA plan sponsors by the average annual wages of employees.

Figure 7: Percentage of Small Employer 401(k) Plan Sponsors and SIMPLE IRA Plan Sponsors by Average Annual Wages of Employees in 2009

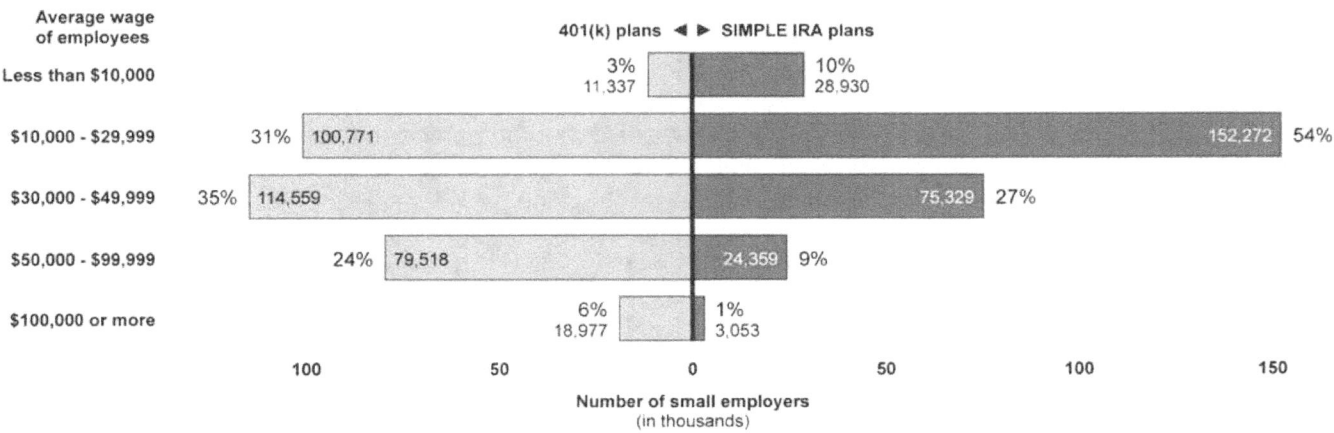

Source: GAO analysis of Labor and IRS data

Finally, while SIMPLE IRA plans were the most common plan type along with 401(k) plans, they made up a smaller proportion of the overall plan contributions. Contributions to SIMPLE IRA plans in 2009 amounted to $4.3 billion, or 11 percent of the total contributions made by small employers and their employees into the plan types GAO analyzed. By contrast, 401(k) contributions amounted to $29.2 billion, or 76 percent of all contributions.

Plan Complexity and Resource Constraints Were Most Frequently Cited Barriers to Retirement Plan Sponsorship

Many Small Employers Find Retirement Plans Complex and Burdensome to Start and Administer

Small employers and other stakeholders[40] identified various plan options, administration requirements, fiduciary responsibilities, and top-heavy testing requirements as complex and burdensome, often citing these factors as barriers to sponsoring retirement plans or as reasons for terminating them.

Plan options and administration requirements: Small employers and other stakeholders said that plan options and administration requirements are frequently complex and burdensome and discourage some small employers from sponsoring a plan. For example, some small employers and retirement experts said that the number of plan types and features make it difficult for small employers to compare and choose plans. Representatives of a plan service provider said that too many plan options overwhelmed small employers, making it more difficult for them to choose a plan and, ultimately, less likely that they will sponsor one. Some stakeholders also described the administrative burden of plan paperwork, such as reviewing complicated quarterly investment reports or complying

---

[40]Stakeholders included small employers, retirement experts, organizations representing small employers, retirement plan service providers, representatives of the accounting profession, and officials at Labor and IRS.

with federal reporting requirements—like those associated with required annual statements—as particularly burdensome. For example, one small employer with a DB plan described a dense and highly technical quarterly investment report for his plan that ran 50 pages, making it difficult to glean summary financial information about the plan. Another small employer who previously sponsored a 401(k) with a company match said the amount of required plan paperwork, including generating annual reports, was a key reason he terminated it. Stakeholders also identified interim amendment requirements as burdensome for plan administration. Plan sponsors generally submit plan documentation to IRS periodically to ensure that plans are up to date and compliant with relevant federal statutes and regulations. However, when statutes and regulations change, some sponsors may be required to modify plan documentation and resubmit their plan documents to IRS. Some stakeholders, including small employers, a small business advocacy organization, and plan service provider, said that complying with interim amendment requirements can be costly and time consuming for small employers. IRS has recognized that interim amendment requirements pose a burden to plan sponsors.[41] However, an IRS official noted that most small employer plans are likely based on plan designs that are preapproved by IRS, and interim amendment requirements are likely to entail little administrative burden for most small employer sponsors.[42]

Fiduciary responsibilities: A number of stakeholders indicated that understanding and carrying out a sponsor's fiduciary responsibilities with respect to their qualified retirement plans presents significant challenges to some small employers. Plan sponsors may qualify as fiduciaries under ERISA, for example, if they have discretionary authority or control over the management of the plan or control the plan assets. Fiduciaries have a number of responsibilities, such as the duty to act prudently, in the sole interest of the participants and beneficiaries, and to diversify the investments of the plan.[43] Some small employer sponsors found the selection of investment fund options for their plans particularly challenging. A small employer with a 401(k) plan described the difficulties of selecting

---

[41]Advisory Committee on Tax Exempt and Government Entities, *Ninth Report of the ACT*, June 9, 2010.

[42]According to the IRS official, pre-approved plans are designed to satisfy certain IRS requirements and have fewer filing requirements.

[43]29 U.S.C. § 1104(a).

appropriate investment options, with an appropriate balance of risk, for a workforce that includes younger and older workers. A number of small business advocates and retirement experts said that not all small employers have an adequate understanding of their fiduciary duties and are not always aware of all their responsibilities under the law. For example, a retirement expert said that small employers that do not consult with plan professionals often lack the time and expertise to understand complicated fiduciary rules under ERISA. One service provider explained that some small employers mistakenly believe that all fiduciary responsibilities and liabilities are transferred to a service provider when they are hired. Another expert noted that some small employers have an exaggerated sense of the liabilities that being a fiduciary carries, and may avoid sponsoring a plan out of fear of being sued by their employees.

Top-heavy requirements: Top-heavy requirements are most likely to affect smaller plans (fewer than 100 participants), according to IRS. A number of stakeholders said compliance with the requirements is often burdensome and poses a major barrier to plan sponsorship for small employers. Small employers with high employee turnover may face an even greater likelihood of becoming top-heavy. According to some experts, employee turnover alone can force some small employers out of compliance with top-heavy requirements as they replace departing employees. Over time, rank-and-file employees separate and take their plan assets with them, while long-term employees, such as business owners or executives, continue to contribute to the plan, eventually leading to a top-heavy imbalance of plan assets. For example, one small employer with a 401(k) plan stated that, because two of the four owners had worked for the company for about 25 years and their retirement accounts made up the majority of the total plan assets in the 401(k) plan, the plan had become top-heavy.

To comply with the top-heavy requirements, sponsors of certain plans[44] are required to test their plans annually. An employer's failure to make certain adjustments to a plan deemed top-heavy can result in it losing its tax-qualified status and the associated tax advantages for the employer and employees. A number of stakeholders stated that top-heavy compliance is confusing and can pose significant burdens on some small

---

[44]Generally, DC plans, DB plans, and SEP IRA plans are subject to the top-heavy rules. SIMPLE IRA plans and some safe harbor 401(k) plans are exempt. 26 U.S.C. § 416(g)(4)(G) and (H).

GAO-12-326 Small Employer Plan Sponsorship

employers. For example, some retirement experts said that small employers whose plans are found to be top-heavy may encounter a number of additional costs in the effort to make their plans compliant, such as hiring a plan professional to make corrections to the plan document and instituting a minimum top-heavy employer contribution for all participating rank-and-file employees. According to one expert, in some cases, the costs of mandatory contributions to employees' accounts may prevent owners from making contributions to their own retirement accounts, and may make some small employers reluctant to sponsor a plan, or may drive those that sponsor a plan to terminate it. Sponsors can avoid top-heavy testing by adopting a safe harbor 401(k) plan with no additional contributions, which is not subject to top-heavy requirements. However, safe harbor 401(k) plans require the employer to make either specified matching contributions or a minimum 3 percent contribution to each participant's account. According to representatives of the accounting professional, the additional cost to the employer of required contributions under a 401(k) safe harbor plan may offset the advantages of sponsoring such a plan.

Federal Guidance Is Available to Address the Complexities Associated with Plan Sponsorship but May Lack Visibility among Small Employers

Federal agencies provide guidance that can assist small employers in addressing some of the challenges of starting and maintaining retirement plans. Labor and IRS, often in collaboration with SBA, have produced publications, conducted workshops, and developed online resources, among other efforts, to assist small employers in understanding options, requirements, and responsibilities of running a plan. For example, Labor and IRS jointly published a guide that compares various features of different plan types, including IRA, DC, and DB plans. Both agencies have also developed websites and online tools to help small employers navigate plan information and make informed decisions about plan options. For example, IRS's Retirement Plans Navigator is a key component of its education efforts for small employers and is designed for employers that are less likely to hire a service provider. According to IRS, the navigator is intended to lead a novice through basic information on retirement plans and compliance. Similarly, Labor, in collaboration with the American Institute of Certified Public Accountants (AICPA), developed an interactive website highlighting small employer retirement options. The website introduces employers to a number of plan options from simpler IRA plans to more complex automatic enrollment 401(k) plans, and describes the advantages and features of various plan types. According to Labor, employers with as few as two employees can find options using the tool.

However, a number of stakeholders suggested that many small employers are unaware of federal resources on retirement plans. For example, the Advisory Committee on Tax Exempt and Government Entities (ACT)[45] recognized that, despite the numerous IRS retirement plan resources available, many small employers and other stakeholders in the small business community are unaware of these resources.[46] ACT indicated these resources could go a long way in addressing the needs of the small employers were it not for their lack of visibility. The lack of visibility of federal guidance on small employer plan options may be due, in part, to difficulties in finding useful, relevant information across federal websites. For example, while Labor's webpage on small employer retirement plan options contains links to relevant topics, such as compliance assistance, participants' rights and fiduciary responsibilities, it is easy to navigate away from but difficult to return to the content developed for small employers because there is no consistent page navigation menu for small employer information. Furthermore, while the Labor website includes guidance on selecting and monitoring plan service providers, there is no link to the guidance on the small employer plan options page. IRS's Retirement Plans Navigator is located on a separate website from the rest of the agency's online plan resources for small employers. When navigating from the page on small employer retirement plan resources on IRS's main portal to the agency's Retirement Plans Navigator, a message alerts users that they are leaving the IRS website and entering another government website. IRS officials noted that small employers who participated in focus groups on IRS plan resources reported challenges to understanding plan-based information when navigating these resources. Furthermore, Labor and IRS present their online content separately, which makes it necessary for an employer to navigate both agencies' websites to gather complete information about starting and maintaining a retirement plan. For example, to review information on fiduciary responsibilities, users must visit Labor's website, and to review information on nondiscrimination and top-heavy testing, users must visit IRS's site. Neither agency maintains a central web portal for all information relevant to small employer plan sponsorship, though such portals exist for federal information resources in other areas such as

---

[45]The ACT was established in 2001 to provide an organized public forum for IRS to receive regular input on exempt organization and employee plan policy.

[46]Advisory Committee on Tax Exempt and Government Entities, *Ninth Report of the ACT* (June 15, 2011).

healthcare.[47] Consolidating Internet-based services and information is also consistent with one of the purposes of the E-Government Act of 2002 to promote interagency collaboration in providing electronic government services.[48]

Small Employers Identified Lack of Financial Resources, Time, and Personnel as Deterrents to Sponsoring Retirement Plans

Small employers that lack sufficient financial resources, time, and personnel may be unwilling or unable to sponsor retirement plans. In particular, stakeholders stated that plan sponsorship may be impractical for smaller or newer firms that are unable to undertake the commitment to sponsor a plan. For example, one expert noted that the first priority of a small employer is remaining in business, and this focus may preclude sponsoring a retirement plan as a benefit to employees until the firm becomes more established.

Financial resources: Small employers, especially those with lower profit margins or an unstable cash flow, could be less willing or less able to sponsor a retirement plan because of the one-time costs to start a plan and the ongoing costs involved with maintaining the plan. These costs can result from start-up activities, complying with reporting and testing requirements, and fees paid to an outside party for administration tasks. Stakeholders stated that these expenses can make sponsoring a plan unappealing. For example, one small employer stated that as a new business owner, she thinks it is better for her business to proceed cautiously and avoid adding to her fixed cost structure. Additionally, any requirement for small employers to match employee contributions or to make mandatory contributions to an employee's account can also increase costs. Further, small employers stated that general economic uncertainty makes them reluctant to commit to such long-term expenses and explained that they needed to reach a certain level of profitability before they would consider sponsoring a plan. For example, one small employer stated that he wanted to be able to expect consistent profits over several years before he would consider investing in a plan. Another small employer stated that she wanted to triple her business revenue to a little less than $1 million before she would consider sponsoring a retirement plan.

---

[47]For example, see: http://www.healthcare.gov/.

[48]Pub. L. No. 107-347, 116 Stat. 2899.

Time and personnel: Some small employers stated they may not have sufficient time to administer a retirement plan themselves or lacked the personnel to take on those responsibilities. For example, one small employer said that he was not prepared to assume the burden of managing a plan as he thought it would require almost daily attention and did not have the staff to devote to it. Further, a plan service provider described how the focus of the small employer would not be on absorbing the additional time that starting and maintaining a plan would require. Additionally, a plan sponsor employer stated that, since her business did not have a dedicated human resources person or accountant, she performed these duties herself, as she would ultimately be responsible for any mistakes. Further, small employers may not have time to develop the expertise to investigate or choose financial products, select the best investment options, or track their performance. For example, one small employer described how business owners without the financial expertise to compare and select from among different plan options would likely find the experience intimidating.

Small Employers Report That Insufficient Incentives and Lack of Employee Demand Discourage Plan Sponsorship

Some small employers stated that they may be less likely to sponsor a retirement plan if they do not perceive sufficient benefits to the business or themselves. For example, several small employers stated that their firms sponsored retirement plans in order to provide the business owners with a tax-deferred savings vehicle. One small employer stated that his firm evaluated the plan annually in order to determine whether it continues to benefit the owners. A service provider observed that the cost of mandatory contributions—such as those associated with safe harbor 401(k) plans—can discourage small employers, since the cost of the contributions can outweigh the benefit to the owners.

Low employee demand for an employer-sponsored retirement plan may also be a challenge for small employers. For example, a number of small employers stated that employees prioritized health care benefits over retirement benefits. One small employer thought that, given the limited funds available to contribute towards benefits, his employees would prefer those resources be applied toward lowering the employees' share of health insurance premiums. Small employers emphasized that offering health care benefits was necessary to attract quality employees. Further, one small employer stated that his employees perceived a more immediate need for health care benefits, while perceiving retirement benefits as a future concern. Additionally, some small employers, such as those who described having younger workforces, stated that their employees were less concerned about saving for retirement and, as a result, were not demanding retirement benefits. Other small employers told us that employees, particularly those with low pay, do not have any interest in retirement benefits because they live paycheck to paycheck and are less likely to have funds left over to contribute to a plan. For example, one small employer discontinued his plan when too few of his employees—most of whom he described as low wage—participated in the plan. Another small employer noted that even senior-level managers in his business did not participate in the plan. However, a retirement expert stated that, while some employees might not be interested in participating in a retirement plan, he believed the perceived lack of demand to be exaggerated. He added that he believed some businesses may use lack of employee demand as an excuse when the small employer was not interested in sponsoring a plan.

Plan Service Providers Help Small Employers Meet Some but Not All Retirement Plan Needs

A number of small employers indicated that they use plan service providers to address various aspects of plan administration, which enabled them to overcome some challenges of starting and maintaining a plan. For example, one small employer said his service provider addresses his plan testing requirements and educates employees about the plan. Another employer noted that her business would not have the time or the expertise to administer their plan without a service provider. A third employer stated that he would not be able to administer a plan without the assistance of a service provider to help navigate the complexity of plan administration.

Some stakeholders said that service providers offer small employers plan administration solutions by providing basic, affordable plan options. For example, one service provider said a small employer could sponsor a plan for an administrative fee as low as $1,200 annually. They and other retirement industry representatives said they are able to provide plan options at affordable rates because they market and administer IRS pre-approved standard plans in high volume, thereby reducing the costs of administration. Even so, while some small employers said the fees service providers charge were affordable, others said they were too high. Further, some stakeholders pointed to other limitations of using service providers, such as the difficulties of choosing a provider, setting up a new plan through a provider, and switching to a new provider, as well as the significant plan responsibilities that remain with the sponsor. For example, a small employer described the process of finding a service provider and setting up a plan as particularly difficult, especially for an employer with little knowledge of retirement plans or experience in working with a service provider. Another small employer said she was not satisfied with the services of her current service provider but would not consider switching to a new one because of the administrative hardships that would entail. Finally, as representatives of the accounting profession noted, even with the assistance of a service provider, small employer sponsors often continue to have significant plan responsibilities, such as managing plan enrollments and separations, and carrying out their fiduciary duties.

Proposed Options to Spur Plan Sponsorship Target Simplification, Incentives, and Education

Stakeholders Proposed Simplifying Requirements and Increasing Tax Credits to Encourage Plan Sponsorship

Stakeholders provided several suggestions targeted at addressing some of the administrative and financial challenges they believed inhibited plan sponsorship.[49] These proposals, which they said could reduce complexity and ease administrative and financial burdens for small employer plan sponsors, included simplifying plan administration rules, revising or eliminating top-heavy testing, and increasing tax credits.

Simplify plan administration requirements: Several stakeholders suggested proposals that could simplify plan administration requirements and ease administrative burdens for small employers. For example, representatives of a large service provider stated that there is a need for simplification of existing rules and processes for retirement plans and proposed easing nondiscrimination and top-heavy testing requirements as an example. Similarly, several small employers said that federal regulators should strive for simplicity in requirements governing plan administration. A small employer who sponsored a 401(k) plan suggested reducing the amount of paperwork as an example. Another small

---

[49]The key proposals discussed in this report are not exhaustive, and we did not attempt to quantify the costs and benefits of each proposal or their potential effectiveness in encouraging small employer plan sponsorship.

employer who sponsored a 401(k) plan said federal regulators should "just keep it simple." One proposal from a national small business association would simplify plan requirements by reducing the frequency of statements sent to certain plan participants, from quarterly to once per year, and allowing some required disclosures to be made available solely online. Another proposal, advocated by IRS, would simplify plan requirements by streamlining interim amendment requirements—an aspect of plan administration that stakeholders identified as particularly burdensome for some small employers.[50] Each year since 2004, IRS has published a cumulative list of changes in plan qualification requirements that must be incorporated by plan sponsors. An IRS official stated that IRS is proposing to replace a requirement for some interim amendments with a requirement for notices to be sent directly to employees. These notices would explain how a plan intends to comply with changes to relevant laws and regulations and could reduce the burden for plan sponsors by reducing the number of times plan documents must be amended. The amendments that would be subject to the less-stringent requirement would be those triggered by changes to laws and regulations but that do not affect plan benefits.

Revise or eliminate top-heavy testing: A number of stakeholders proposed revising or eliminating top-heavy testing to ease administrative and financial burdens. For example, representatives of the accounting profession told us that top-heavy testing is duplicative because there are other plan testing requirements intended to detect and prevent plan discrimination against rank-and-file employees.[51] The representatives and officials of a large service provider told us lack of plan participation or high turnover among a business's rank-and file employees frequently cause plans sponsored by small employers to become top-heavy.[52] As a result,

---

[50]IRS identified interim amendments as a focus for simplification in its 2011 annual work plan and is considering proposed changes. See Cumulative List of Changes in Plan Qualification Requirements reports, IRS Notices 2011-97, 2010-90 and 2009-98.

[51]For example, some plans must conduct nondiscrimination testing—in addition to top-heavy testing—to ensure that the contributions or benefits provided under the plan do not discriminate in favor of highly compensated employees. See 26 U.S.C. § 401(a)(4) and 26 C.F.R. §§ 1.401(a)(4)-1 through 1.401(a)(4)-4. GAO did not specifically assess duplication between top-heavy and nondiscrimination testing requirements.

[52]However, some plans that may be sponsored by small employers, including SIMPLE IRA plans and certain safe harbor 401(k) plans, are not subject to top-heavy rules. 26 U.S.C. § 416(g)(4)(G) and (H).

the representatives said top-heavy testing should be revised or eliminated.

Increase tax credits: Some stakeholders believed that tax credits, in general, are effective in encouraging plan sponsorship and that larger tax credits could encourage more small employers to sponsor plans. However, a stakeholder cautioned that the credits must be sufficient to offset the costs of plan sponsorship, which a service provider said can amount to $2,000 or more per year. Currently, small employers may claim an annual tax credit of up to $500 based on plan startup costs for each of the first 3 years of starting a qualified plan.[53] A national organization representing small employers cited tax credits as a top factor in an employer's decision to sponsor a plan; however, an organization official said the likelihood of an employer doing so often depends on whether the tax credit offsets a significant portion of administrative and startup costs of sponsoring plans. Some small employers stated that larger tax credits could ease the financial burden of starting a plan by offsetting plan-related costs, thus creating greater incentives for an employer to sponsor a plan. Other stakeholders said that existing plan startup tax credits are insufficient to encourage plan sponsorship. Officials at another national small business association cautioned that short term tax credits do not provide sufficient incentives for a small employer to make the long-term commitment of sponsoring a plan. Similarly, one small employer who sponsored both 401(k) and DB plans said there needs to be a larger

---

[53]For information on the credit for small employer pension plan startup costs, see 26 U.S.C. § 45E.

incentive for the small employer to sponsor a plan because starting and maintaining plans can be expensive.[54]

Stakeholders Said More Education and Outreach Are Needed to Increase Awareness of Plan Options and Requirements

Numerous stakeholders agreed that the federal government could conduct more education and outreach to inform small employers about plan options and requirements; however, opinions varied on the appropriate role for the federal government in this area.

A retirement expert said that the federal government can do more to educate consumers about retirement plans and improve general financial literacy. Officials of a service provider to small businesses stated that, because clients are generally not aware of the retirement plan options available to them, the federal government should provide more education and outreach to improve awareness of the plan types available and rules that apply to each. Another large service provider mentioned the federal government should provide educational materials that help small employers find quality service providers. In addition, in its 2011 report, ACT made numerous recommendations calling for better publicity of IRS resources. According to the report, the committee recommended, among other things, that IRS explore potential partnerships with community organizations and plan service providers to enhance the visibility of IRS resources for small employers.

Although several small employers agreed on the need for more education and outreach about plan options and requirements, opinions varied on the extent to which the federal government should provide these services. For example, a representative of a small employer believed the federal

---

[54]However, any increase in tax incentives would have to be balanced by the loss of revenue to the federal government. Increasing tax credits to subsidize retirement plan sponsorship costs for small employers would generally reduce the amount of federal tax revenue collected. For example, the Administration's fiscal year 2013 budget proposed a system of automatic IRAs that would offer small employers who adopt an automatic IRA a tax credit of up to $500 for the first year and $250 for the second year. These employers would be entitled to an additional credit of $25 per enrolled employee, up to $250 for 6 years. In addition, the Administration's 2013 budget included a proposal to double the maximum tax credit for small employer plan startup costs, from $500 to $1,000 per year, for 3 years, and also extend the duration of the tax credit from 3 years to 4 years if a small employer also adopts a new qualified retirement plan, SEP, or SIMPLE during the first 3 years of starting an automatic IRA arrangement. This proposal would increase the potential maximum tax credit from $1,500 to $4.000. According to Administration's estimates, these proposals were projected to represent about $15 billion in reduced revenue over 10 years, starting in 2013.

government could provide more educational materials that are easy to understand. Another small employer said the federal government should focus education and outreach on service providers instead of on small employers. Conversely, some small employers said the federal government should have a limited role or no role in providing education and outreach efforts.

Other Options to Encourage Plan Sponsorship Would Require Broader Reforms

There are a number of domestic pension reform proposals from public policy organizations, as well as practices in other countries, that include features, such as asset pooling, that potentially reduce administrative and financial burdens and could boost retirement plan sponsorship among small employers. By pooling funds, small employers realize economies of scale because plan administration is simplified and administrative costs and asset management fees are reduced. Pooling also creates larger plans, which are more likely to attract service providers that previously may have found it uneconomical to service smaller individual plans. One proposal by the Economic Policy Institute, which incorporates the concept of asset pooling, would create a federally managed and federally guaranteed national savings plan.[55] Generally, participation in the program would be mandatory for workers,[56] and employers and employees would be required to make equal contributions totaling 5 percent of employees' earnings. Funds would be pooled and professionally managed, and benefits would be paid out in the form of annuities to ensure that workers do not outlive their savings.[57] In addition, Automatic IRAs—which are individual IRAs instead of employer-sponsored plans—are another proposal that draws from several elements of the current retirement system: payroll-deposit saving, automatic enrollment, and IRAs. The automatic IRA approach would provide

---

[55]Teresa Ghilarducci, *Guaranteed Retirement Accounts Toward Retirement Income Security*, Economic Policy Institute, Briefing Paper #204 (Nov. 20, 2007).

[56]Under this proposal, workers participating in equivalent or better employer DB plans where contributions are at least 5 percent of earnings and benefits take the form of life annuities would be exempt from participating in the guaranteed retirement accounts program.

[57]Recent legislation introduced in Congress, the Small Businesses Add Value for Employees Act (SAVE Act), would also build on the concept of asset pooling by establishing multiple employer plans for small employers, in which separate small employers would pool their resources to offer a single plan. See H.R. 1534, 112th Cong. (introduced Apr. 14, 2011).

GAO-12-326 Small Employer Plan Sponsorship

employers that do not sponsor any retirement plans with a mechanism that allows their employees to save a portion of their pay in an IRA. For most employees, payroll deductions would be made by direct deposit, and enrollment would be automatic unless employees choose to opt out of participation.[58]

However, as we reported in 2009, some of these proposals that call for broader systemic reforms pose other trade-offs.[59] For example, proposals that mandate participation would increase plan sponsorship and coverage for workers. However, mandatory participation may create burdens for some employers, and employers might compensate for the costs of contributing to workers' retirement plans by reducing workers' wages and other benefits. Proposals that guarantee investment returns can protect workers from market fluctuations and can ensure a minimum level of benefits; however, significant costs to the government might result if the guarantee were unsustainable. In addition, proposals that simplify and centralize 401(k) plans may require new regulatory and oversight efforts, and compliance-related costs could be passed on to employers, workers, and taxpayers in general.

Retirement systems in other countries also use asset pooling and other features that reduce administrative and financial burdens for small employers and could spur plan sponsorship. For example, the United Kingdom's National Employment Savings Trust (NEST), launched in 2011, features low fees for participating employers and employees and default investment strategies for plan participants. NEST also permits plan participants to take their retirement accounts with them throughout their working life, which eliminates ongoing administration of those accounts by former employers when a worker leaves a company. As we previously reported, the predominant pension systems in the Netherlands and Switzerland pool plan assets into pension funds for economies of scale and for lower plan fees.[60] Denmark's pension system also pools

---

[58]J. Mark Iwry and David C. John, *Pursuing Universal Retirement Security Through Automatic IRAs*, Retirement Security Project, No. 2009-03 (2009),

[59]GAO, *Private Pensions: Alternative Approaches Could Address Retirement Risks Faced by Workers but Pose Trade-offs*, GAO-09-642 (Washington, D.C.: July 24, 2009).

[60]GAO-09-642.

plan assets[61] and uses existing tax data to calculate plan contributions, further lowering administrative costs for small employers.

Conclusions

Despite efforts by the federal government to develop new plan designs and to increase tax incentives to spur plan formation and retirement saving generally, sponsorship remains low among small employers. To some extent, it would be expected that sponsorship rates for small employers would be somewhat lower than for larger employers partly because of the heavy "churn" of small business formation and dissolution. However, small employers' sponsorship rates remain far below those of larger firms. If a complete picture of sponsorship by small employers were available—including information on small employers that sponsor SEP IRA plans, which is lacking because IRS currently does not have a means to collect these data—IRS and Labor would be better able to target their research and outreach efforts.

Small employers continue to face a variety of challenges to starting and maintaining retirement plans, including obtaining useful information about the large menu of available plan options, managing administrative requirements that small employers reported as burdensome and overly complex, and drawing upon small employers' often limited resources to administer and finance a plan. While increased competition among plan service providers may result in more affordable options and plans that are easier to start and maintain, options for many small employers may remain out of reach.

Federal agencies have a key role to play in understanding and addressing the barriers to plan sponsorship and to spur sponsorship among small employers by conducting research and conducting education and outreach to small employers. Labor and IRS already provide small employers with a great deal of online information. However, much of the information is scattered among a variety of websites and portals in a largely uncoordinated fashion. A small employer with little knowledge of retirement plan options is forced to navigate multiple sources to retrieve relevant information and may be discouraged from doing so. Increased collaboration and more comprehensive strategic

---

[61]GAO *Private Pensions: Changes Needed to Better Protect Multiemployer Pension Benefits*, GAO-11-79 (Washington, D.C.: Oct. 18, 2010).

planning between these agencies could enhance outreach and education efforts to more small employers. For example, Labor and IRS could reach out to small employers by utilizing SBA's extensive network of field offices and by entering into partnerships with public and private organizations. More fundamentally, a coordinated review by the relevant agencies of existing plan designs and their effectiveness in spurring plan sponsorship and participation could help agencies evaluate and develop options that mitigate the barriers to small employer plan sponsorship.

Recommendations for Executive Action

Department of Labor

To address the need to strengthen the retirement security of employees at small businesses and to build on interagency data-sharing agreements already in place, we recommend that the Secretary of Labor convene an interagency task force with representatives from Treasury, IRS, and SBA, and other agencies deemed appropriate, to review, analyze, and address the challenges facing small business retirement security in the United States. The aim of this taskforce would be to develop strategies and arrangements for the agencies to routinely and systematically coordinate their existing research, education, and outreach efforts to foster small employer plan sponsorship. Specifically, this body should focus on, but not be limited to, the following goals:

- Conduct plan research on the characteristics associated with small businesses that are more or less likely to sponsor a retirement plan (including employer-sponsored IRA plans) to support agencies' education and outreach efforts to small employers and provide Congress and the public with information about plan coverage among them.

- Evaluate and develop proposals for mitigating barriers to small employer retirement plan sponsorship, including an assessment of the cost effectiveness of existing plan designs—with regard to the expansion of coverage, and the potential to provide an adequate retirement income, as necessary--and the appropriateness of alternative plan designs.

- Create a single web portal to centralize federal agencies' retirement plan information to enhance the visibility and usefulness of federal guidance on plans for small employers.

Department of the Treasury

Considering the lack of information on the number and characteristics of sponsors of SEP IRA plans, as well as their performance in improving retirement security, the Secretary of the Treasury should direct the Commissioner of the Internal Revenue Service to consider modifications to tax forms, such as Forms W-2 or 5498, that would allow IRS to gather complete and reliable information about these plans.

Agency Comments and Our Evaluation

We provided a draft of the report to Labor, Treasury, IRS, Commerce, and SBA for review and comment. Agencies generally agreed with our recommendations. Only Labor provided a written response (see app. VII). Labor, Treasury, IRS, and SBA also provided technical comments, which we incorporated as appropriate. Commerce did not provide comments.

In its written response, Labor generally agreed with the findings and conclusions of the report. Labor also noted that, since 1995, the agency has developed various initiatives to provide education and outreach to the small business community—particularly in the context of retirement saving and financial literacy—by partnering with SBA, the U.S. Chamber of Commerce, and other entities to target small employers. Labor cited these and other efforts as progress in response to of our recommendation for a taskforce that would analyze and address the challenges facing small business retirement security, stating that Labor remains committed to continuing its existing coordination efforts with respect to plan research and developing proposals for mitigating barriers to small business plan sponsorship.

However, Labor disagreed with our recommendation to create a unified web portal to centralize retirement plan information for small employers, expressing concerns about its necessity. Specifically, Labor noted that an SBA website, http://www.business.gov, currently serves as the central portal for information—including information about retirement plans—relevant to small employers. However, none of the stakeholders we interviewed during this report—including Labor and SBA officials—identified http://www.business.gov as a resource of retirement plan information for small employers. Further, in reviewing http://www.business.gov, we found the retirement plan information consisted primarily of links that send users to websites maintained by

Labor. We did not find links to or information regarding any IRS retirement plan guidance, including the Retirement Plans Navigator—the agency's key online retirement plan tool for small employers—or http://www.choosingretirementsolution.org, Labor's online retirement plan tool for small employers. However, even if http://www.business.gov contained links to all available federal guidance on retirement plans for small employers, it is not clear how it would increase the visibility of the guidance among small employers because so few small employers and other stakeholders we spoke with appeared to be aware of its existence. Thus, while we commend Labor for its existing coordination efforts, we continue to believe that there are additional benefits to be gained by consolidating information on retirement plans for small employers into a single, easy-to-use source—an initiative that would also appear to be consistent with the administration's interest in information technology consolidation and in encouraging agencies to conduct their missions more effectively.

Finally, in its written response, Labor cited BLS's 2010 National Compensation Survey, which found that an estimated 45 percent of establishments employing fewer than 100 workers offered a retirement plan to their workers. This is not necessarily inconsistent with our estimate of 14 percent of small employers sponsoring some form of retirement plan, given the different units of analysis used. While the National Compensation Survey used "establishment" as its unit of analysis, we chose to use "firms" for the purposes of this study. There are important differences between an establishment and a firm. For example, according to BLS's definition, an establishment is a single economic unit at a single physical location. Thus, an establishment can be a business at a single physical location or a branch of a larger company operating multiple branches and the characteristics of each branch is measured as a separate business instead of in the aggregate. On the other hand, for this study, we defined a firm as a complete, for-profit, independent business with 1 to 100 employees. As a result, Labor's estimate comprises a broader population of employers beyond the small employers we examined. Further discussion of our methodology can be found in appendix I.

As agreed with your offices, unless you publicly announce the contents of this report earlier, we plan no further distribution until 30 days from the report date. At that time, we will send copies to the Secretary of Labor, Secretary of the Treasury, the Secretary of Commerce, the SBA

Administrator, and other interested parties. This report will also be available at no charge on the GAO website at http://www.gao.gov.

If you or your staff have any questions regarding this report, please contact Charles Jeszeck at (202) 512-7215 or jeszeckc@gao.gov. Contact points for our Offices of Congressional Relations and Public Affairs can be found on the last page of this report. Key contributors are listed in appendix VIII.

Charles Jeszeck
Director, Education, Workforce
  and Income Security

Appendix I: Objectives, Scope, and Methodology

Information Regarding the Rates of Small Business Employees Who Do Not Have Access to a Retirement Plan, Based on BLS and Census Data

In the body of this report, we present a range for the rate of employee access to retirement plans. According to the Congressional Research Service (CRS), the differences in the estimates regarding employee access to retirement plans between information obtained from Bureau of Labor Statistics (BLS) and the Census Bureau may stem from the different populations used in the surveys. BLS's National Compensation Survey (NCS) is conducted among a nationally representative sample of private-sector business establishments. The term establishment usually refers to a single place of business at a particular location. An establishment might be a branch or a small operating unit of a larger firm. The Census Bureau's Current Population Survey (CPS) is conducted among a nationally representative sample of households. Employer characteristics are reported at the level of the firm, which may include more than one establishment. CRS has reported that, in any given year, the NCS can reasonably be expected to show a higher rate of retirement plan participation than the CPS because the business owners and benefits specialists who are interviewed for the NCS might have greater knowledge about the retirement benefits they sponsor than the household members who are interviewed for the CPS. However, CRS has noted that the gap in Census and BLS estimates has grown over time, further complicating the process of estimating both the proportion of workers without employer-sponsored retirement plans and the trend in retirement plan participation rates.[1]

Data Sources and Development of the Analytic Data Set

To perform this work, we combined and analyzed 2009 data from the Department of Labor's (Labor) Form 5500 database, the Internal Revenue Service's (IRS) Information Returns Processing (IRP) database, and the IRS Compliance Data Warehouse database (CDW) to obtain information on what would make a small employer more or less likely to sponsor a retirement plan, descriptive statistics on small employer retirement plan sponsors and nonsponsors, and descriptive statistics on the types of retirement plans sponsored by small employers. The Form 5500 database provided information on defined benefit (DB) and defined contribution (DC) plans, and the publicly available data was downloaded directly from Labor's website: http://www.dol.gov/ebsa/foia/foia-5500.html. The IRP database provided information on employer-sponsored SIMPLE

---

[1] John J. Topoleski, *Pension Sponsorship and Participation: Summary of Recent Trends*, Congressional Research Service (Washington, D.C.: September 2009)

IRA and SARSEP IRA plans and was provided by the IRS officials in the
Tax-Exempt Governmental Entity Employment Plans division. The CDW
database provided the characteristics regarding the universe of small
employers with 100 or fewer employees and was provided by IRS officials
with the Statistics of Income (SOI) division. We assessed the reliability of
the Form 5500, the IRP, and the CDW data generally and of data
elements that were critical to our analyses and determined that they were
sufficiently reliable for our analyses.

Our unit of analysis was the small employer, as identified by its employer
identification number (EIN). For the purposes of this study, we defined a
small employer as an independently owned and operated for-profit firm
with at least 1 employee and no more than 100 employees. This definition
excluded agricultural businesses, such as farms, as well as tax-exempt
organizations, such as nonprofits and government entities. This definition
also excluded subsidiary for-profit firms.

To prepare the Form 5500 data in advance of combining the data with the
other datasets, we screened out any plans that were not entered in the
Form 5500 or Form 5500-SF as "single employer plans," those that did
not have a plan year beginning date in 2009, as well as screened out any
plans that had entries in the Welfare Benefit Codes. Our analysis did not
consider small employers that only participated in multiple employer
plans, in which two or more employers maintain a single plan, or
multiemployer plans, in which a joint plan is maintained under a collective
bargaining agreement between at least one employee organization and
more than one employer. As individual employers are not considered
sponsors of multiple employer plans and multiemployer plans, including
these plans was considered beyond the scope of this report.[2] We then
matched the Form 5500 data and the IRP data with the CDW data using
the EIN in common. Any matches between a small employer in the CDW
database and a plan in either the Form 5500 or IRP database classified
the small employer as one that sponsored the plan while any small
employers that did not match with a plan were classified as nonsponsors.

---

[2]Under Title I of ERISA, a plan sponsor "in the case of a plan established or maintained by
two or more employers or jointly by one or more employers and one or more employee
organizations" is "the association, committee, joint board of trustees, or other similar group
of representatives of the parties who establish or maintain the plan." 29 U.S.C. §
1002(16)(B)(iii).

Data Analysis of Small Employer Plan Sponsorship

We developed bivariate and multivariate regression models to estimate the likelihood that a small employer would sponsor a retirement plan using the following small employer characteristics: the number of employees, the annual average wage of the employees, the industry using the 2007 North American Industry Classification System (NAICS) with a depth of two digits, and the region in which the small employer resided as defined by the Census Bureau. For results of the regression model, see appendix VI. The regression model did not include the age of the business as a variable in the model. It is difficult to measure this variable because, over time, a small employer may change its EIN. For example, some small employers change their business structure,[3] which may also require the business to obtain a new EIN. It would be challenging to track businesses over time with changes to the EIN.

In addition to the regression model, we produced a descriptive statistical analysis of small employer characteristics using cross-tabulations of the following characteristics: the number of employees, the annual average salary of the employees, the industry using the NAICS with a depth of two digits, and the state in which the small employer is located. The ranges used for the characteristics identifying the number of employees and average annual wages were established using the statistical spreads identified by the regression model.

Data Analysis of Plan Type

In order to categorize the plan type for plans in the Form 5500 database, we took an approach similar to a model followed by Labor.[4] We ranked the Pension Benefit Codes using the order established by Labor and assigned a plan type according to the first ranked code found in the Pension Benefits Code variable string using the following order:

---

[3]Business structures may include a sole proprietorship, a partnership, a corporation, an S corporation, or a limited liability company (LLC).

[4]U.S. Department of Labor, *Retirement Private Pension Plan Bulletin: Abstract of 2008 Form 5500 Annual Reports* (December 2010).

Table 1: 5500 Retirement Plan Type and Feature Assignment Order by Pension Benefit Code

Category	Plan type	Characteristic code	Variable
Defined benefit (DB)	Cash Balance Plan	1C	
	Other DB Plan	1D,1F,IG	5500: TYPE_PENSION_BNFT_CODE SF 5500 (short form): SF_TYPE_PENSION_BNFT_CODE
Defined contribution (DC)	Profit Sharing Plan	2E	
	Stock Bonus Plan	2I	
	Target Benefit Plan	2B	
	Money Purchase Plan	2C	
	Other DC plans	2F, 2D, 2O, 2P, 2R	
Feature	401(k)	2J	

Source: GAO analysis of Labor Form 5500 pension plan characteristic codes.

To categorize any remaining plans, we performed a string search of the plan names using the Plan Name variable in each form as follows:

- If "cash balance," then Cash Balance Plan.

- If "defined benefit," then "Other DB."

- If "profit sharing," then Profit Sharing Plan.

- If "stock bonus," then Stock Bonus Plan.

- If "target benefit," then Target Benefit Plan.

- If "money purchase," then Money Purchase Plan.

- If "401(k)," then Profit Sharing Plan.

- If "employee stock" or "stock ownership" or "ESOP," then "other DC plan."

Finally, with any further unassigned plans, we examined the Participant Account Balance variable for the Form 5500 and Form 5500-SF and assigned any plans with balances greater than "0" as "Other Defined Contribution."

Once all of the Form 5500 plans had been assigned a plan type, an additional search occurred to look through all of the plans to find those with a plan characteristic code 2J or variations on the string search "401(k)" in the plan name. The additional search produced a breakdown of which plan types had the 401(k) plan feature.[5]

After combining the CDW data with the IRP and Form 5500 data and after categorizing each matched plan in the Form 5500 database, matched small employers were categorized as sponsoring a type of DC plan or DB plan from the Form 5500 database or a SIMPLE IRA or a SARSEP IRA from the IRP database. We produced a frequency count of each plan type sponsored by a small employer that sponsored a single plan. Any small employers that sponsored multiple plans were excluded from the plan type frequency count due to challenges in identifying the correct plan to assign that small employer or in double counting the small employer.[6] Additionally, we produced descriptive statistics identifying the plan types sponsored by small employers using the small employer characteristics of number of employees, average annual salary, industry type, and state of residence. Finally, we produced descriptive output information on the plan contributions categorized by the plan type, as well as cross tabulated with the small employer characteristics.

Analysis of Small Employer Challenges

To examine challenges encountered by small employers when starting and maintaining retirement plans, we interviewed 27 small employers across the country. Nineteen employers sponsored a retirement plan, and 8 employers did not sponsor a plan. We held nine small group interviews in five major cities across the country: Atlanta, Boston, Chicago, Los Angeles, and Washington, D.C. We also held individual interviews with five employers that were not able to attend group interviews in those cities. We selected these cities for the purposes of geographic dispersion, which allowed us to leverage GAO field office resources in planning and conducting interviews. To identify our interview sites, we selected urban centers instead of less-populated areas because a wider variety of businesses and industries are located in or near cities.

---

[5]For this study, we classified 401(k) as a plan type.

[6]About 19,000 small employers sponsored multiple plans, which represent about 3 percent of the overall sponsor population.

To select small employers, stakeholders recommended that we contact local Chambers of Commerce to identify and invite local small employers for interview participation. We discussed our study and details of our planned group interviews with officials at the Small Business Administration and the U.S. Chamber of Commerce. Chamber officials assisted us in contacting local Chambers of Commerce in the cities identified above. We discussed our study and details of the group interviews with local chamber officials, who agreed to help us with our data collection and host the interviews. We worked with the local chamber contacts to obtain lists of chamber members who were small employers, and we invited these members—through e-mail messages and phone calls—to participate in our group interviews. The local chambers hosted the interviews and allowed us to use their facilities and conference rooms.

Our interview protocols also sought to identify and interview small employers of varying sizes. The small employers that participated in our interviews represented businesses of varying sizes, up to 65 employees, from various industries and sectors of the economy, including consulting, architecture, health care, light manufacturing, law, marketing, service, and banking. Findings from our interviews with small employers are qualitative in nature and were not meant to be representative of the overall population of small employers nationwide.

In conducting our interviews, we held separate interviews with small employers that sponsored plans and that did not sponsor plans. The interview protocol for both groups was the same. However, the structured data collection instrument—our interview questions—differed between sponsors and nonsponsors. For plan sponsors, our questions focused on factors that influenced their decisions to sponsor retirement plans and challenges they encountered in maintaining retirement plans. For nonsponsors, our questions focused on factors that influenced their decisions not to sponsor retirement plans and challenges that prevented them from starting retirement plans.

To ensure that our questions were easy to understand and captured the necessary information, we conducted pretests with small employers that were members of the Washington, D.C., Chamber of Commerce. In addition, we tested our interview protocols to ensure that participation would not be burdensome for small employers. Using the pretest results, we consolidated some of our questions. However, because no substantive changes were made to our interview questions, we included results from the pretests in the results obtained from the interviews in other cities to formulate our findings.

Our examination of challenges encountered by small employers when
starting and maintaining retirement plans also included interviews with
retirement experts, including individuals representing public policy research
organizations and attorneys specializing in retirement benefits,
organizations representing small employers, retirement plan service
providers, representatives of the accounting profession, as well as federal
agency officials.

Analysis of Proposed Options to Address Small Employer Challenges

To compile options that could address challenges encountered by small
employers when starting and maintaining retirement plans for their workers,
in addition to interviews with small employers throughout the country, we
interviewed a range of retirement experts, including individuals
representing public policy research organizations and attorneys
specializing in retirement benefits, organizations representing small
employers, retirement plan service providers, and representatives of the
accounting profession. Stakeholders also included officials at Labor and
IRS, who provided information on the role of federal agencies in conducting
oversight of federal plan requirements. In our interviews with stakeholders,
we gathered information on proposed options that could address small
employers' plan-related challenges. In addition, we reviewed relevant
portions of federal laws and regulations and proposed legislation on new
plan types. The key proposals discussed in our report are not exhaustive,
and we did not attempt to quantify the costs and benefits of each proposal
or their potential effectiveness in encouraging small employer plan
sponsorship.

To identify domestic pension reform proposals that could address
challenges encountered by small employers in sponsoring plans, we
conducted a review of available literature and proposals published by
public policy organizations. We selected examples that included a plan
feature—asset pooling—that was common across many proposals. To
identify examples of proposed legislation on new types of retirement
plans, we searched electronic databases for proposed federal legislation
that included provisions related to retirement plans for small employers
and selected a recent proposal that builds on the concept of asset
pooling. For examples of international retirement plan features that
address challenges to small employer plan sponsorship, we drew from
prior GAO reports on international retirement plan systems and selected
examples that included features that could assist small employers.

We conducted this performance audit from October 2010 to March 2012
in accordance with generally accepted government auditing standards.
Those standards require that we plan and perform the audit to obtain

sufficient, appropriate evidence to provide a reasonable basis for our findings and conclusions based on our audit objectives. We believe that the evidence obtained provides a reasonable basis for our findings and conclusions based on our audit objectives.

Appendix II: Some Retirement Plans Available to Small Employers

Table 2 is based on guidance produced by Labor and the IRS to educate small employers about their retirement plan options. This guidance, titled "Choosing a Retirement Solution for Your Small Business," can be found at http://www.dol.gov/ebsa/pdf/choosing.pdf. The content of this table is reproduced from the Labor/IRS publication without alteration, with the following exceptions: GAO updated some dollar amounts to reflect changes made for 2012, where applicable (specifically, the maximum annual contributions to the defined contribution plans and SEP IRA plans, and the maximum compensation upon which contributions to non-DB plans may be based), reordered the columns, and omitted information about payroll deduction IRA plans, which are beyond the scope of this review. GAO did not independently verify the legal accuracy of the information contained in the table.

Table 2: Some Retirement Plans Available to Small Employers

	IRA-Based Plans		Defined Contribution Plans				Defined Benefit
	SEP	SIMPLE IRA Plan	Traditional 401(k)	Safe Harbor 401(k)	Automatic Enrollment 401(k)	Profit Sharing	
Key Advantage	Easy to set up and maintain.	Salary reduction plan with little administrative paperwork.	Permits high level of salary deferrals by employees without annual discrimination testing.	Permits high level of salary deferrals by employees. Also safe harbor relief for default investments.	Provides high level of participation and permits high level of salary deferrals by employees. Also safe harbor relief for default investments.	Permits employer to make large contributions for employees.	Provides a fixed, pre-established benefit for employees.
Employer Eligibility	Any employer with one or more employees.	Any employer with 100 or fewer employees that does not currently maintain another retirement plan.	Any employer with one or more employees.	Any employer with one or more employees.	Any employer with one or more employees.	Any employer with one or more employees.	Any employer with one or more employees.
Employer's Role	May use IRS Form 5305-SEP to set up the plan. No annual filing requirement for employer.	May use IRS Forms 5304-SIMPLE or 5305-SIMPLE to set up the plan. No annual filing requirement for employer. Bank or financial institution handles most of the paperwork.	No model form to establish this plan. Advice from a financial institution or employee benefit adviser may be necessary. A minimum amount of employer contributions is required. Requires annual non-discrimination testing to ensure plan does not discriminate in favor of highly compensated employees.	No model form to establish this plan. Advice from a financial institution or employee benefit adviser may be necessary. A minimum amount of employer contributions is required. Annual filing of Form 5500 is required.	No model form to establish this plan. Advice from a financial institution or employee benefit adviser may be necessary. Annual filing of Form 5500 is required. Some plans require annual non-discrimination testing to ensure they do not discriminate in favor of highly compensated employees.	No model form to establish this plan. Advice from a financial institution or employee benefit adviser may be necessary. Annual filing of Form 5500 is required.	No model form to establish this plan. Advice from a financial institution or employee benefit adviser would be necessary. Annual filing of Form 5500 is required. An actuary must determine annual contributions.
Contributors To The Plan	Employer contributions only.	Employee salary reduction contributions and employer contributions.	Employee salary reduction contributions and maybe employer contributions.	Employee salary reduction contributions and employer contributions.	Employee salary reduction contributions and maybe employer contributions.	Annual employer contribution is discretionary.	Primarily funded by employer.

	IRA-Based Plans		Defined Contribution Plans				Defined Benefit
	SEP	SIMPLE IRA Plan	Traditional 401(k)	Safe Harbor 401(k)	Automatic Enrollment 401(k)	Profit Sharing	
Maximum Annual Contribution (per participant). See *http://www.irs.gov/ep* **for annual updates.**	Up to 25% of compensation[a] but no more than $50,000 for 2012.	**Employee:** $11,500 in 2012. Additional contributions up to $2,500 can be made by participants age 50 or over. **Employer:** Either match employee contributions 100% of first 3% of compensation (can be reduced to as low as 1% in any 2 out of 5 yrs.); or contribute 2% of each eligible employee's compensation[b].	**Employee:** $17,000 in 2012. Additional contributions can be made by participants age 50 or over up to $5,500. **Employer/Employee Combined:** Up to the lesser of 100% of compensation[a] or $50,000 for 2012. Employer can deduct (1) amounts that do not exceed 25% of aggregate compensation for all participants and (2) all salary reduction contributions.	**Employee:** $17,000 in 2012. Additional contributions can be made by participants age 50 or over up to $5,500. **Employer/Employee Combined:** Up to the lesser of 100% of compensation[a] or $50,000 for 2012. Employer can deduct (1) amounts that do not exceed 25% of aggregate compensation for all participants and (2) all salary reduction contributions.	**Employee:** $17,000 in 2012. Additional contributions can be made by participants age 50 or over up to $5,500. **Employer/Employee Combined:** Up to the lesser of 100% of compensation[a] or $50,000 for 2012. Employer can deduct (1) amounts that do not exceed 25% of aggregate compensation for all participants and (2) all salary reduction contributions.	Up to the lesser of 100% of compensation[a] or $50,000 in 2012. Employer can deduct amounts that do not exceed 25% of aggregate compensation for all participants.	Annually determined contribution.
Contributor's Options	Employer can decide whether to make contributions year-to-year.	Employee can decide how much to contribute. Employer must make matching contributions or contribute 2% of each employee's compensation.	Employee can decide how much to contribute pursuant to a salary reduction agreement. The employer can make additional contributions, including matching contributions as set by plan terms.	Employee can decide how much to contribute pursuant to a salary reduction agreement. The employer must make either specified matching contributions or a 3% contribution to all participants.	Employees, unless they opt otherwise, must make salary reduction contributions specified by the employer. The employer can make additional contributions, including matching contributions as set by plan terms.	Employer makes contribution as set by plan terms.	Employer generally required to make contribution as set by plan terms.
Minimum Employee Coverage Requirements	Must be offered to all employees who are at least 21 years of age, employed by the employer for 3 of the last 5 years and had compensation of $550 for 2012.	Must be offered to all employees who have earned income of at least $5,000 in any prior 2 years, and are reasonably expected to earn at least $5,000 in the current year.	Generally, must be offered to all employees at least 21 years of age who worked at least 1,000 hours in a previous year.	Generally, must be offered to all employees at least 21 years of age who worked at least 1,000 hours in a previous year.	Generally, must be offered to all employees at least 21 years of age who worked at least 1,000 hours in a previous year.	Generally, must be offered to all employees at least 21 years of age who worked at least 1,000 hours in a previous year.	Generally, must be offered to all employees at least 21 years of age who worked at least 1,000 hours in a previous year.

	IRA-Based Plans		Defined Contribution Plans				Defined Benefit
	SEP	SIMPLE IRA Plan	Traditional 401(k)	Safe Harbor 401(k)	Automatic Enrollment 401(k)	Profit Sharing	
Withdrawals, Loans & Payments	Withdrawals permitted anytime subject to federal income taxes, early withdrawals subject to an additional tax.	Withdrawals permitted anytime subject to federal income taxes, early withdrawals subject to an additional tax.	Withdrawals permitted after a specified event occurs (e.g., retirement, plan termination, etc.) subject to federal income taxes. Plan may permit loans and hardship withdrawals; early withdrawals subject to an additional tax.	Withdrawals permitted after a specified event occurs (e.g., retirement, plan termination, etc.) subject to federal income taxes. Plan may permit loans and hardship withdrawals; early withdrawals subject to an additional tax.	Withdrawals permitted after a specified event occurs (e.g., retirement, plan termination, etc.) subject to federal income taxes. Plan may permit loans and hardship withdrawals; early withdrawals subject to an additional tax.	Withdrawals permitted after a specified event occurs (e.g., retirement, plan termination, etc.). Plan may permit loans; early withdrawals subject to an additional tax.	Payment of benefits after a specified event occurs (e.g. retirement, plan termination, etc.).
Vesting	Contributions are immediately 100% vested.	Employee salary reduction contributions and employer contributions are immediately 100% vested.	Employee salary reduction contributions are immediately 100% vested. Employer contributions may vest over time according to plan terms.	Employee salary reduction contributions and most employer contributions are immediately 100% vested. Some employer contributions may vest over time according to plan terms.	Employee salary reduction contributions are immediately 100% vested. Employer contributions may vest over time according to plan terms.	May vest over time according to plan terms.	May vest over time according to plan terms.

Sources: Department of Labor and IRS.

a Maximum compensation on which 2012 contributions can be based is $250,000.

b Maximum compensation on which 2012 employer 2 % nonelective contributions can be based is $250,000.

Appendix III: IRS Form 5498 IRA Contribution Information

2828	☐ VOID	☐ CORRECTED	

TRUSTEE'S or ISSUER'S name, street address, city, state, and ZIP code	1 IRA contributions (other than amounts in boxes 2-4, 8-10, 13a, and 14a) $	OMB No. 1545-0747 2011 Form 5498	**IRA Contribution Information**
	2 Rollover contributions $		
	3 Roth IRA conversion amount $	4 Recharacterized contributions $	Copy A For Internal Revenue Service Center
TRUSTEE'S or ISSUER'S federal identification no.	PARTICIPANT'S social security number	5 Fair market value of account $	6 Life insurance cost included in box 1 $
PARTICIPANT'S name		7 IRA ☐ SEP ☐ SIMPLE ☐ Roth IRA ☐	File with Form 1096.
		8 SEP contributions $	9 SIMPLE contributions $	For Privacy Act and Paperwork Reduction Act Notice, see the 2011 General Instructions for Certain Information Returns.
Street address (including apt. no.)		10 Roth IRA contributions $	11 Check if RMD for 2012 ☐
		12a RMD date	12b RMD amount $
City, state, and ZIP code		13a Postponed contribution $	13b Year	13c Code
		14a Repayments $	14b Code
Account number (see instructions)			

Form 5498   Cat. No. 50010C   Department of the Treasury - Internal Revenue Service

Do Not Cut or Separate Forms on This Page — Do Not Cut or Separate Forms on This Page

Source: IRS

Appendix IV: Small Employer Plan Sponsorship Rate by Industry

In analyzing small employer retirement plan sponsorship by industry, we found that small employers in heath care and manufacturing were most likely to sponsor a retirement plan, while small employers in the food and hospitality industry were least likely to sponsor a plan. See figure 8 for the sponsorship rate by industry and table 3 for a sample list of businesses contained within each industry type.

Figure 8: Small Employer Plan Sponsorship Rate by Industry Type in 2009

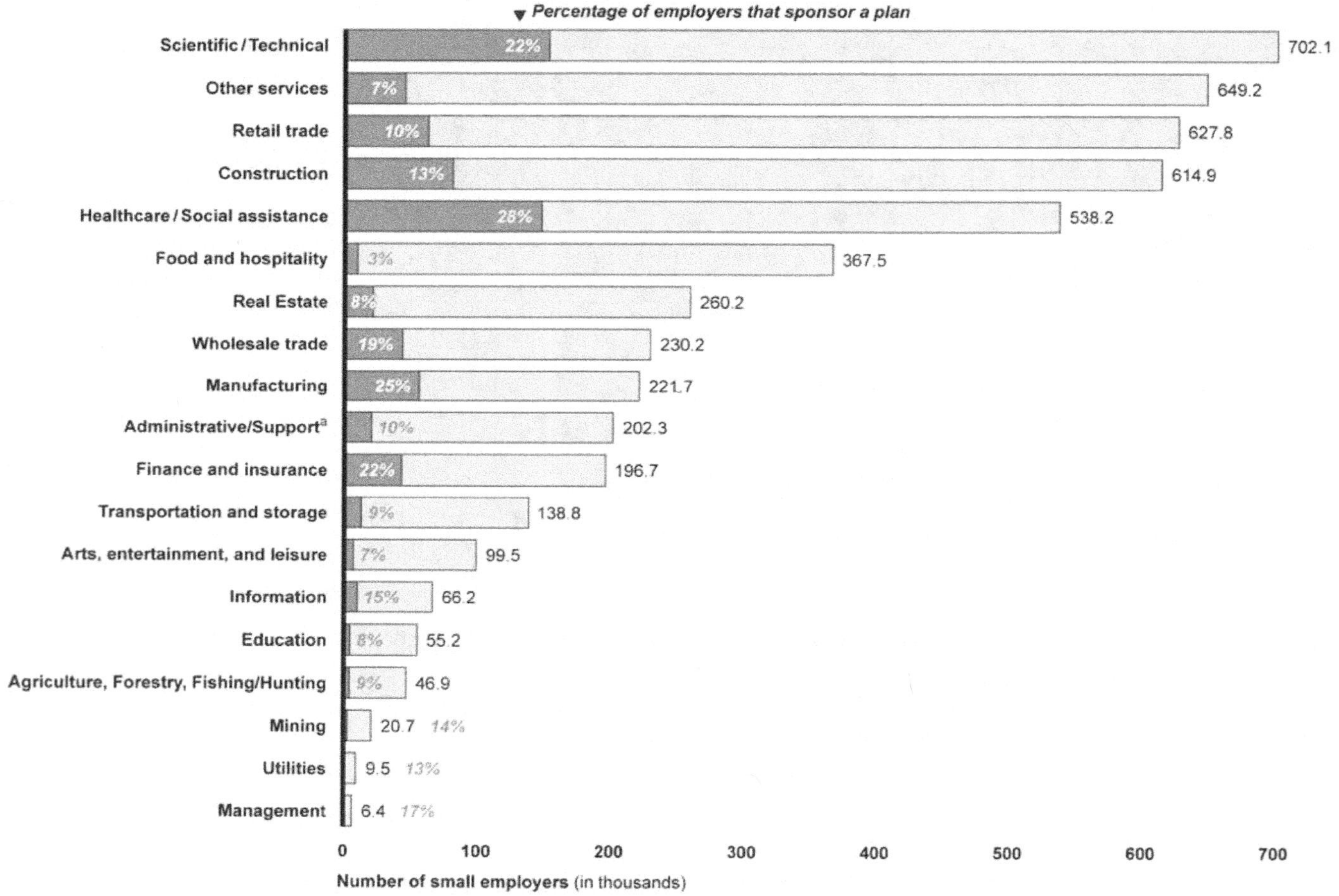

▼ *Percentage of employers that sponsor a plan*

Industry	Percentage	Number (thousands)
Scientific / Technical	22%	702.1
Other services	7%	649.2
Retail trade	10%	627.8
Construction	13%	614.9
Healthcare / Social assistance	28%	538.2
Food and hospitality	3%	367.5
Real Estate	8%	260.2
Wholesale trade	19%	230.2
Manufacturing	25%	221.7
Administrative/Support[a]	10%	202.3
Finance and insurance	22%	196.7
Transportation and storage	9%	138.8
Arts, entertainment, and leisure	7%	99.5
Information	15%	66.2
Education	8%	55.2
Agriculture, Forestry, Fishing/Hunting	9%	46.9
Mining	14%	20.7
Utilities	13%	9.5
Management	17%	6.4

Number of small employers (in thousands)

Source: GAO analysis of Labor and IRS data

Note: All employers counted in the table employed from 1 to 100 employees.

Table 3: Composition of Industry Classifications

Industry category	Examples
Scientific/technical/ professional	Legal services, accounting, architecture, engineering, computer systems design, scientific research, advertising, public relations
Other services	automotive repair and maintenance, barber shops and beauty salons, civic and professional organizations, funeral homes, laundry services, personal goods repair and maintenance
Retail trade	Automobile dealers, book and music stores, building material and garden equipment dealers, clothing stores, electronics and appliance stores, food and beverage stores, gasoline stations, sporting good stores
Construction	Construction of buildings, heavy and civil engineering construction, specialty trade contractors
Heath care/social assistance	Child day care services, hospitals, nursing and residential care facilities, offices of health care practitioners (physicians, dentists, chiropractors, optometrists, etc), outpatient and home health care centers
Food and hospitality	Restaurants and taverns, accommodation services
Real estate and rental and leasing	Real estate agents and brokers, automotive equipment rental and leasing, consumer good rental
Wholesale trade	Durable and nondurable goods wholesalers, wholesale electronics market
Manufacturing	Computer and electronic product manufacturing, food manufacturing, machinery and metal product manufacturing, petroleum and chemical manufacturing, textile product mills
Administrative support and waste management and remediation services	Office administrative services, employment services, travel arrangement and reservation services, waste collection, waste treatment and disposal
Finance and insurance	Commercial banking, funds and trusts, savings institutions, securities and commodities exchanges, insurance carriers
Transportation and warehousing	Air transportation, couriers and messengers, postal service, sightseeing transportation, transit and ground passenger transportation, water transportation, warehousing and storage
Arts, entertainment, and recreation	Spectator sports, amusement parks, gambling, promoters and agents
Information and communication	Broadcasting, data processing, motion picture and sound recording, publishing industries, telecommunications
Education	Computer and management training, educational support services, technical and trade schools
Agriculture, forestry, fishing/hunting	Animal and crop production, fishing, forestry, hunting, trapping
Mining, quarrying, and oil and gas extraction	Mining, oil and gas extraction
Utilities	Electric power, natural gas distribution, water and sewage
Management	Management of companies and enterprises, offices of bank holding companies

Source: U.S. Bureau of Labor Statistics, 2007 North American Industry Classification System, last revised February 28, 2011.

Note: This list contains examples for illustrative purposes and is not a complete list.

Appendix V: Small Employer Plan Sponsorship Rate by State in 2009

State	Sponsorship percentage	Census region
Alabama	11.7	South
Alaska	14.0	West
Arizona	12.1	West
Arkansas	10.6	South
California	13.0	West
Colorado	13.3	West
Connecticut	19.7	Northeast
Delaware	17.3	South
District Of Columbia	22.5	South
Florida	9.5	South
Georgia	11.4	South
Hawaii	16.0	West
Idaho	12.6	West
Illinois	14.4	Midwest
Indiana	15.4	Midwest
Iowa	18.1	Midwest
Kansas	15.5	Midwest
Kentucky	14.4	South
Louisiana	13.3	South
Maine	14.2	Northeast
Maryland	17.6	South
Massachusetts	19.2	Northeast
Michigan	16.2	Midwest
Minnesota	18.0	Midwest
Mississippi	9.8	South
Missouri	13.4	Midwest
Montana	13.8	West
Nebraska	16.8	Midwest
Nevada	10.1	West
New Hampshire	18.0	Northeast
New Jersey	14.3	Northeast
New Mexico	11.9	West
New York	12.8	Northeast
North Carolina	12.8	South
North Dakota	16.4	Midwest
Ohio	18.1	Midwest

State	Sponsorship percentage	Census region
Oklahoma	11.6	South
Oregon	15.5	West
Pennsylvania	16.9	Northeast
Rhode Island	16.4	Northeast
South Carolina	11.5	South
South Dakota	14.6	Midwest
Tennessee	11.7	South
Texas	10.5	South
Utah	10.2	West
Vermont	18.1	Northeast
Virginia	14.9	South
Washington	13.8	West
West Virginia	11.9	South
Wisconsin	19.6	Midwest
Wyoming	12.6	West
Puerto Rico	5.0	NA
Other U.S. territories	**5.5**	
American Samoa		NA
Federated States Of Micronesia		NA
Guam		NA
Northern Mariana Islands		NA
Virgin Islands		NA
National Small Employer Average, including Puerto Rico and other U.S. territories	13.8	NA

Source: GAO analysis of Labor and IRS data.

Appendix VI: Regression Results

Table 4: Results of Bivariate Analysis

Category	Percentage of businesses	Percentage of businesses sponsoring retirement programs	Odds ratio from bivariate model	Significance of odds ratio
Overall U.S. small business	100.0%	13.8%	1.00	
	(N=5,344,369)	(N=735,098)		
Employee count				
1 to 4	51.9%	5.5%	0.20	**
5 to 11	24.9%	17.6%	1.49	**
12 to 25	13.6%	25.9%	2.60	**
25 to 100	9.7%	31.3%	3.39	**
Average wage per employee				
Less than $10,000	31.8%	2.8%	0.12	**
$10,000 - $29,999	43.6%	12.6%	0.84	**
$30,000 - $49,999	15.0%	28.4%	3.16	**
$50,000 - $99,999	7.2%	34.5%	3.81	**
$100,000 or greater	2.5%	25.8%	2.23	**
NAICS				
11 = Agriculture, Fishing, Foresting	0.9%	9.1%	0.63	**
21 = Mining	0.4%	14.4%	1.05	*
22 = Utility	0.2%	12.8%	0.92	**
23 = Construction	11.5%	13.2%	0.95	**
31 = Manufacturing (incl. 33 and 34)	4.2%	25.3%	2.21	**
42 = Whole Sale Trade	4.3%	18.9%	1.49	**
44 = Retail Trade (incl. 45)	11.8%	10.0%	0.67	**
48= Transportation/Warehousing	2.6%	9.20%	0.63	**
51 = Information	1.2%	15.3%	1.14	**
52 = Finance and Insurance	3.7%	21.8%	1.80	**
53 = Real Estate and Rental and Leasing	4.9%	8.2%	0.55	**
54 = Professional, Scientific, and Technical Services	13.1%	21.9%	1.96	**
55 = Management of Companies and Enterprises	0.1%	16.9%	1.28	**
56 = Administrative and Support and Waste Management and Remediation Services	3.8%	10.1%	0.70	**
61 = Education Services	1.0%	8.4%	0.57	**
62 = Healthcare	10.1%	27.5%	2.73	**
71 = Art, Entertainment, and Recreation	1.9%	7.3%	0.49	**
72 = Accommodation and Food Service	6.9%	2.7%	0.16	**

Category	Percentage of businesses	Percentage of businesses sponsoring retirement programs	Odds ratio from bivariate model	Significance of odds ratio
81 = Other Services	12.2%	7.0%	0.44	**
99 = Invalid	0.2%	1.7%	0.11	**
00 = Missing	0.4%	1.6%	0.10	**
Census Bureau regions and divisions				
Region 1 = Northeast	20.0%	15.3%	1.17	**
Division 1: New England	5.3%	18.4%	1.45	**
CT	1.2%	19.7%	1.55	**
ME	0.6%	14.2%	1.04	*
MA	2.3%	19.2%	1.51	**
NH	0.5%	18.0%	1.38	**
RI	0.4%	16.5%	1.23	**
VT	0.3%	18.1%	1.39	**
Division 2: Middle Atlantic	14.7%	14.2%	1.05	**
NJ	3.3%	14.3%	1.05	**
NY	7.4%	12.8%	0.91	**
PA	4.0%	16.9%	1.29	**
Region 2 = Midwest	21.8%	16.3%	1.30	**
Division 3: East North Central	14.3%	16.4%	1.28	**
IN	1.9%	15.4%	1.15	**
IL	4.3%	14.4%	1.06	**
MI	3.0%	16.2%	1.22	**
OH	3.3%	18.1%	1.40	**
WI	1.9%	19.6%	1.54	**
Division 4: West North Central	7.5%	16.1%	1.22	**
IA	1.1%	18.1%	1.39	**
KS	1.0%	15.5%	1.15	**
MN	2.0%	18.0%	1.39	**
MO	2.0%	13.4%	0.97	**
NE	0.7%	16.8%	1.27	**
ND	0.3%	16.4%	1.23	**
SD	0.4%	14.6%	1.07	**

　　　　　　　　　　　　　　　　　　　GAO-12-326 Small Employer Plan Sponsorship

Category	Percentage of businesses	Percentage of businesses sponsoring retirement programs	Odds ratio from bivariate model	Significance of odds ratio
Region 3 = South	33.6%	11.9%	0.78	**
Division 5: South Atlantic	19.0%	12.2%	0.85	**
DE	0.3%	17.3%	1.31	**
DC	0.2%	22.5%	1.82	**
FL	6.7%	9.5%	0.65	**
GA	2.8%	11.4%	0.81	**
MD	1.8%	17.6%	1.35	**
NC	2.8%	12.8%	0.92	**
SC	1.3%	11.5%	0.82	**
VA	2.5%	14.9%	1.10	**
WV	0.5%	11.9%	0.85	**
Division 6: East South Central	4.8%	12.1%	0.85	**
AL	1.3%	11.7%	0.83	**
KY	1.2%	14.4%	1.06	**
MS	0.7%	9.8%	0.68	**
TN	1.6%	11.7%	0.83	**
Division 7: West South Central	9.8%	11.0%	0.76	**
AR	0.9%	10.6%	0.74	**
LA	1.3%	13.3%	0.96	**
OK	1.2%	11.6%	0.82	**
TX	6.5%	10.5%	0.72	**
Region 4 = West	24.0%	13.0%	0.92	**
Division 8: Mountain	7.6%	12.2%	0.86	**
AZ	1.7%	12.1%	0.86	**
CO	2.1%	13.3%	0.96	**
ID	0.6%	12.6%	0.90	**
NM	0.6%	11.9%	0.85	**
MT	0.6%	13.8%	1.00	
UT	1.0%	10.2%	0.71	**
NV	0.7%	10.1%	0.71	**
WY	0.3%	12.6%	0.90	**

Category	Percentage of businesses	Percentage of businesses sponsoring retirement programs	Odds ratio from bivariate model	Significance of odds ratio
Division 9: Pacific	16.4%	13.4%	0.97	**
AK	0.3%	14.0%	1.02	
CA	11.8%	13.0%	0.93	**
HI	0.4%	16.0%	1.20	**
OR	1.5%	15.5%	1.15	**
WA	2.4%	13.8%	1.00	

Source: GAO analysis of Labor and IRS data.

** denotes p-value < 0.01.

* denotes p-value < 0.05.

Table 5: Results of Multivariate Analysis

Category	Odds ratio from multivariate model	p-value	95 percent Wald Confidence Limits (lower)	95 percent Wald Confidence Limits (upper)
Employee count				
1 to 4	0.23	<.0001	0.22	0.23
5 to 11	Ref.			
12 to 25	1.92	<.0001	1.91	1.94
26 to 100	3.13	<.0001	3.10	3.15
Average wage per employee				
Less than $10,000	0.23	<.0001	0.23	0.23
$10,000 - $29,999	Ref.			
$30,000 - $49,999	2.58	<.0001	2.56	2.60
$50,000 - $99,999	3.62	<.0001	3.59	3.66
$100,000 or Greater	3.23	<.0001	3.19	3.28
NAICS				
11 = Agriculture, Fishing, Foresting	0.98	0.2414	0.95	1.01
21 = Mining	1.12	<.0001	1.07	1.17
22 = Utility	0.71	<.0001	0.66	0.76
23 = Construction	Ref.			
31 = Manufacturing (incl. 33 and 34)	1.63	<.0001	1.60	1.65
42 = Whole Sale Trade	1.45	<.0001	1.43	1.47
44 = Retail Trade (incl. 45)	1.05	<.0001	1.04	1.06
48 = Transportation/Warehousing	0.77	<.0001	0.75	0.78

Category	Odds ratio from multivariate model	p-value	95 percent Wald Confidence Limits (lower)	95 percent Wald Confidence Limits (upper)
51 = Information	1.20	<.0001	1.17	1.23
52 = Finance and Insurance	2.70	<.0001	2.66	2.74
53 = Real Estate and Rental and Leasing	1.04	<.0001	1.02	1.06
54 = Professional, Scientific, and Technical Services	2.39	<.0001	2.36	2.41
55 = Management of Companies and Enterprises	1.32	<.0001	1.22	1.42
56 = Administrative and Support and Waste Management and Remediation Services	1.03	0.0007	1.01	1.05
61 = Education Services	0.60	<.0001	0.59	0.63
62 = Healthcare	2.59	<.0001	2.56	2.61
71 = Art, Entertainment, and Recreation	0.86	<.0001	0.84	0.88
72 = Accommodation and Food Service	0.29	<.0001	0.29	0.30
81 = Other Services	0.75	<.0001	0.74	0.76
89 = Services, Not Elsewhere Classified	0.35	<.0001	0.30	0.41
00 = Missing	0.41	<.0001	0.36	0.45
Census Bureau regions and divisions				
Division 1: New England	1.37	<.0001	1.35	1.39
Division 2: Middle Atlantic	Ref.			
Division 3: East North Central	1.28	<.0001	1.26	1.29
Division 4: West North Central	1.50	<.0001	1.48	1.52
Division 5: South Atlantic	0.88	<.0001	0.87	0.89
Division 6: East South Central	0.83	<.0001	0.82	0.85
Division 7: West South Central	0.67	<.0001	0.66	0.68
Division 8: Mountain	0.92	<.0001	0.91	0.93
Division 9: Pacific	0.89	<.0001	0.88	0.90

Source: GAO analysis of Labor and IRS data.

Note: "Ref." denotes a reference (or an omitted) category.

Table 6: Results of Block Test

	-2*Log-likelihood	Model explanatory power (Pseudo-R2)	Contribution of block (percent)
Intercept only	4,280,669.8		
Full model	3,190,599.3	0.34	
Models with one block deleted			
Size	3,656,960.9	0.17	14.62
Average wage	3,507,782.2	0.22	9.94
Industry classification (NAICS)	3,316,274.3	0.29	3.94
Geographic location	3,214,590.3	0.33	0.75

Source: GAO analysis of Labor and IRS data.

Appendix VII: Comments from the Department of Labor

U.S. Department of Labor

Assistant Secretary for
Employee Benefits Security Administration
Washington, D.C. 20210

FEB 2 2 2012

Mr. Charles A. Jeszeck
Director, Education, Workforce, and
  Income Security Issues
United States Government Accountability Office
Washington, DC 20548

Dear Mr. Jeszeck:

Thank you for the opportunity to review the Government Accountability Office's (GAO) draft report entitled "Better Agency Coordination Could Help Small Employers Address Challenges to Plan Sponsorship" (GAO-12-326). With regard to the statistical data presented in the report, we think it is important to note that the National Compensation Survey (NCS), conducted by the Bureau of Labor Statistics, is one of the most authoritative sources of information about employee benefits. In 2010[1], the survey found that approximately 45% of small establishments with fewer than 100 workers were offering a retirement plan to their workers.

Background

Encouraging small businesses to establish retirement plans has been a focus of the Department's *Retirement Savings Education Campaign* since it began in 1995. We recognized the challenges small businesses face and worked to address those challenges through education and outreach. Congress then incorporated this focus of our campaign into a statutory mandate to educate small employers under the 1997 Saver Act. We expanded our efforts with the development of the *Choosing a Retirement Solution Campaign* (for small businesses without a plan) in 2000 and the *Fiduciary Education Campaign* (for small businesses with a plan) in 2004. The title of your report, "Better Agency Coordination Could Help Small Employers Address Challenges to Plan Sponsorship," and the language used throughout do not reflect the excellent cooperation and partnerships we have established and maintained with the Department of Treasury, Internal Revenue Service (IRS), Small Business Administration (SBA), Labor's Small Business Programs Office, American Institute of Certified Public Accountants (AICPA) and other partners necessary to reach the target audience. In order to maximize limited resources, we constantly work with these partners to reach small businesses. We highlight events that bring awareness to saving and financial literacy, such as America Saves Week, Financial Literacy Month and National Save for Retirement Week, to bring greater visibility to our announcements of new materials, tool and outreach events.

---

[1] U.S. Bureau of Labor Statistics, National Compensation Survey: Employee Benefits in the United States, March 2010, Bulletin 2752. Table 1, Establishments offering retirement and health care benefits: private industry workers.

We began our campaign focusing on small businesses by partnering with the SBA and the U.S. Chamber of Commerce to target those businesses. When we began receiving feedback from the small businesses that they looked to their accountants for help in determining if they should offer plans, what type of plans to offer, and for assistance in setting them up, we initiated a partnership with the AICPA to educate their members about the retirement plan options for small businesses. Members of the AICPA joined the local workshops we conduct in coordination with the IRS and helped promote the events and our materials. A successful example of our collaboration is a video developed with members of the AICPA, some of their small business clients, and the employees of these businesses, who talk about their experience in selecting various plan types and provide the peer perspective.

Additionally, we developed and launched an interactive website, http://www.choosingaretirementsolution.org/, in conjunction with the AICPA that helps small employers determine which plan options may be appropriate for them. The user answers a few questions about their situation (such as how many employees they have, whether they want to make contributions, and/or want their employees to contribute, etc.) and then it provides those plan options that are most suitable for their needs. It then provides links to more detailed information on each of those options. The site contains a chart comparing key features of all options available. We received so much demand for a print version of this chart that we included it in our *Choosing a Retirement Solution* publication.

EBSA continues its efforts to expand these campaigns and provide comprehensive and current materials in a variety of formats. Together with the IRS and Treasury, we developed a series of publications and educational materials geared to small businesses that describe all of the plan options available to small businesses and the highlights of each option. We provide workshops and webcasts on this topic in conjunction with the IRS and work with the SBA to make our information and upcoming events available to the intended audience. The SBA promotes all of our events through web postings, blast emails, tweets, blogs, and promotion through their regional offices including regional newsletters. We also contribute a column for IRS' monthly electronic newsletter for small businesses that provides updates on new guidance, web tools, and upcoming seminars and workshops.

We also conduct annual webcasts to reach the small business audience we cannot reach in person at our workshops due to limited resources. On these webcasts we are joined by the IRS and AICPA as well as The Electronic Payment Association (NACHA) who discusses how direct deposit will make it possible to save for retirement. We work closely with the SBA, DOL's Small Business Programs Office and local chambers of commerce along with state CPA societies, local Society for Human Resource Management chapters and other organizations to promote the webcasts and workshops. We have partnered with the Consumer Federation of America to help highlight small business retirement solutions as part of America Saves Week.

Finally, our *Fiduciary Education Campaign* assists small businesses once they have established a retirement plan and is intended to increase awareness and understanding of the basic fiduciary responsibilities related to operating a retirement plan. The issues addressed cover the key responsibilities for the plan, including those that the small business owner is responsible for, and mistakes we frequently see in our enforcement efforts that can be avoided if aware of the responsibilities. Once again, we developed publications in conjunction with the IRS and conduct full day seminars with the IRS to discuss the key areas of the law and both agencies' voluntary correction programs. Annually, we also conduct a two part webcast series with the IRS.

Recommendations

With regard to your recommendation to convene an interagency taskforce with representatives from Treasury, IRS and SBA and other agencies deemed appropriate to review, analyze and address the challenges facing small business retirement security in the United States, we believe the partnerships highlighted above have made significant progress towards educating and encouraging small business owners to offer a retirement plan to their employees and providing assistance to them once they do offer a plan. We are committed to continuing our coordination with the named agencies with respect to plan research and proposals for mitigating barriers to small employer retirement plan sponsorship. However, we do not believe a new web portal focusing on the narrow issue of retirement plans for small business owners is necessary especially in light of the Administration's desire to consolidate web portals and eliminate redundancy. As mentioned above we have launched an interactive website http://www.choosingaretirementsolution.org/, and there is already a site that serves the small business audience, www.business.gov, maintained by the SBA. It is currently the central portal for small businesses to obtain information on a wide variety of issues of interest to small businesses and where small businesses are likely to go for information. The site also attracts service providers to small businesses looking to assist their clients. For years we have posted information on this website and will work with the SBA to ensure that all education and outreach materials developed for small business owners about retirement plan options, fiduciary responsibilities, and self-correction programs by the IRS and EBSA is posted on this site and organized in a user-friendly manner.

For the information we post on our website, we intentionally try not to overwhelm small businesses with a long list of links which make establishing and operating a plan seem too complicated. Rather, we have worked with the IRS to develop publications that provide simple overviews of the law (IRC and ERISA) with a list of resources for more information. On our website we link to the IRS materials included in the resources section of the publications so that a small business owner who is interested in finding out more information has easy access to it. We want to provide information in manageable portions since establishing and operating a plan is voluntary. We have also developed tools, such as tips, a video, and an interactive website, to help small business owners follow through on these actions. The tools have received very positive feedback.

Again, thank you for the opportunity to review the draft report and provide comments. Should you or your staff have any questions concerning the statements included herein, please do not hesitate to contact us.

Sincerely,

Phyllis C. Borzi
Assistant Secretary

Appendix VIII: GAO Contact and Staff Acknowledgments

GAO Contact	Charles Jeszeck, (202) 512-7215 or jeszeckc@gao.gov
Staff Acknowledgments	In addition to the contact named above, individuals making key contributions to this report include David Lehrer, Assistant Director; Edward Bodine, Analyst-in-Charge; Curtis Agor; Kun-Fang Lee; and David Reed. Susan Aschoff, Susan Baker, James Bennett, Michael Brostek, Sarah Cornetto, Cynthia Grant, Catherine Hurley, Anna Kelley, Gene Kuehneman, Karen O'Conor, Dae Park, MaryLynn Sergent, Aron Szapiro, Frank Todisco, James Ungvarsky, and Walter Vance also provided valuable assistance. SOI (IRS) provided valuable assistance in extracting small employer data from the CDW.

GAO's Mission	The Government Accountability Office, the audit, evaluation, and investigative arm of Congress, exists to support Congress in meeting its constitutional responsibilities and to help improve the performance and accountability of the federal government for the American people. GAO examines the use of public funds; evaluates federal programs and policies; and provides analyses, recommendations, and other assistance to help Congress make informed oversight, policy, and funding decisions. GAO's commitment to good government is reflected in its core values of accountability, integrity, and reliability.
Obtaining Copies of GAO Reports and Testimony	The fastest and easiest way to obtain copies of GAO documents at no cost is through GAO's website (www.gao.gov). Each weekday afternoon, GAO posts on its website newly released reports, testimony, and correspondence. To have GAO e-mail you a list of newly posted products, go to www.gao.gov and select "E-mail Updates."
Order by Phone	The price of each GAO publication reflects GAO's actual cost of production and distribution and depends on the number of pages in the publication and whether the publication is printed in color or black and white. Pricing and ordering information is posted on GAO's website, http://www.gao.gov/ordering.htm. Place orders by calling (202) 512-6000, toll free (866) 801-7077, or TDD (202) 512-2537. Orders may be paid for using American Express, Discover Card, MasterCard, Visa, check, or money order. Call for additional information.
Connect with GAO	Connect with GAO on Facebook, Flickr, Twitter, and YouTube. Subscribe to our RSS Feeds or E-mail Updates. Listen to our Podcasts. Visit GAO on the web at www.gao.gov.
To Report Fraud, Waste, and Abuse in Federal Programs	Contact: Website: www.gao.gov/fraudnet/fraudnet.htm E-mail: fraudnet@gao.gov Automated answering system: (800) 424-5454 or (202) 512-7470
Congressional Relations	Katherine Siggerud, Managing Director, siggerudk@gao.gov, (202) 512-4400, U.S. Government Accountability Office, 441 G Street NW, Room 7125, Washington, DC 20548
Public Affairs	Chuck Young, Managing Director, youngc1@gao.gov, (202) 512-4800 U.S. Government Accountability Office, 441 G Street NW, Room 7149 Washington, DC 20548

www.ingramcontent.com/pod-product-compliance
Lightning Source LLC
Chambersburg PA
CBHW081142290526

45795CB00006B/2334